Goodbye Prince Charming

The Journey Back from Disenchantment

Creating the Marriage You've Always Wanted from the Ashes of Storybook Romance

Eileen Silva Kindig

PIÑON PRESS

P.O. Box 35007, Colorado Springs, Colorado 80935

© 1993 by Eileen Silva Kindig
All rights reserved. No part of this publication may be reproduced in any form without written permission from Pinon Press, P. O. Box 35007, Colorado Springs, CO 80935.
Library of Congress Catalog Card Number: 93-11500
ISBN 08910-97465

Some of the anecdotal illustrations in this book are true to life and are included with the permission of the persons involved. All other illustrations are composites of real situations, and any resemblance to people living or dead is coincidental.

Kindig, Eileen Silva.
    Goodbye, Prince Charming : the journey back from disenchantment : creating the marriage you've always wanted from the ashes of storybook romance / Eileen Silva Kindig.
      p. cm.
  ISBN 0-89109-746-5
  1. Marriage. 2. Interpersonal relations.
3. Forgiveness. I. Title.
HQ734.K4827 1993
306.81—dc20   93-11500
                                CIP

Printed in the United States of America

Contents

1 **Someday My Prince Will Come**
   The Cinderella Inside Us All 9

2 **Happily Ever After?**
   Beyond Storybook Romance 21

3 **The Princess Stands Alone**
   The Power of Self-Responsibility 37

4 **Prince Charming in the Sky**
   The Gifts of Mature Spirituality 49

5 **Choosing Trust, Accepting Risk**
   Honoring an Imperfect Union 65

6 **Cycles of Rage**
   Anger as an Avenue Toward Intimacy 81

7 **After the Tears**
   The Grief That Births Compassion 99

8 **Goodbye, Prince Charming**
   Reclaiming Hope Through Forgiveness 111

9 **Ah, Romance!**
   The Bitter and the Sweet 127

10 **Buried Treasure**
    Uncovering a Lasting Love 141

To Eric,
whose faith in me could move mountains

Acknowledgments

It's been said that writing is a solitary task. After emerging from ten months of confinement, I can attest to it. But because I am blessed beyond reason, I always knew that on the other side of my office door awaited a bevy of angels. Gail Butler, Mary Lynn Irish, Gloria Prose, Linda Lavery, Judy Totts, and Jan Leatherman dragged me out for lunches and dinners, broke the silence with welcome phone calls, endured both my euphoria and my hysteria, and generally kept me sane. I'm more grateful than they know.

I'm also thankful for the assistance of the "specialist" angels in my life: Diane Walker and Dan McCormack who provided comic relief; Orvin Oswald, Eric Lohr, and Sherry Ostrowski who tamed my wild computer; Kathy Popio who gave me the courage to be vulnerable; Dr. Bob Banasik who reminded me from the beginning to follow my bliss; Liz Nelson, my favorite librarian who never fails to ask how it's going; Elizabeth Newenhuyse, my friend and colleague who first made me believe this was possible; Mary Dunham of the Village Booksmith who keeps spreading the word; and last, but never least, Traci Mullins, my friend and editor, who's earned her wings a thousand times over.

This experience has been, by turns, exciting, exhilarating, frustrating, and frightening. If a few of the angels hadn't occasionally joined me on my side of the office door I may not have had the courage and the endurance to forge on. To my best friend in all the world, Jessica Jenkins, my husband, Eric, and my daughters, Moira and Caitlin, I send more than gratitude. To you I give my heart and my love — always and forever.

CHAPTER ONE

Someday My Prince Will Come
The Cinderella Inside Us All

❦

Lying on the couch, half asleep, I was startled into awareness by a woman's voice on television saying something to another woman about Prince Charming. By the time I sat up and focused, the commercial had almost ended, leaving me unsure what product it had intended to sell. But it really didn't matter because, in those few brief seconds, it had peddled something far more powerful than any pills or potions.

Oh so subtly it had seduced viewers with a brand of romantic fantasy that women have been buying since the Middle Ages.

Today this fantasy's packaging is every bit as alluring as it ever was (if somewhat more high-tech), its promise as shining—and its results as potentially lethal as a poison apple.

What surprised me is that the two women on the screen selling it were no damsels in distress searching for someone to "take me away from all this." They were young, well-educated professionals, obviously scrambling up the corporate ladder alongside their male counterparts.

They wore their dressed-for-success suits with an air of confident assurance their mothers had struggled to assume back in the consciousness-raising decade of the seventies. And yet, for all their apparent savvy, both unabashedly yearned for that enchanted day when Prince Charming would charge past the fax machine on his white steed and sweep them off to a four-bedroom castle in the suburbs, where they'd live happily ever after with two children, two cars, and two paychecks.

Twenty-five years ago, when I was even younger than the two women in the commercial, I was a hopeless romantic, too. My best friend Patty and I wandered the halls of Saint Mary's High School quoting brooding poetry from the collected works of Rod McKuen, Elizabeth Barrett Browning, and me. While our friends dreamed of weddings with the boys whose class rings they wore wrapped in pastel angora, Patty and I vowed we'd never entertain the notion of marrying a guy from "around here." Who would want to marry someone who'd seen us in our hideous blue-plaid uniforms and knew that the real reason we didn't make editor of the school paper was because we weren't as popular as Christine Leffler? It would take a bold, dashing stranger to win our hearts, we agreed, someone who'd appear one day from some exotic port and sweep us off to a magic kingdom where we'd live the promise of the fairy tale all the days of our lives.

And once upon a time that's exactly what happened to me. Well, sort of anyway. . . .

MY KNIGHT IN SHINING COMBAT BOOTS

I met my husband through the mail. It was 1968, and he was stationed in Vietnam, having been drafted the summer after graduating from Michigan Technological University. I was a junior in high school and a reluctant member of Future Teachers of America, when I was told that the club expected all members to choose the name of a GI from a list of area servicemen published in the *Akron Beacon Journal* and send him a Christmas card.

"Mrs. Robert Smith. No, I don't like that. Too plain," the girl in front of me mused as she perused the list of names taped to the blackboard.

Oh, please, I thought, *let's just get on with it*. It was three below zero outside, and I still had to walk home and tackle three pages of geometry (no small feat, since I wrote the brooding poetry in Sister Marie Michael's geometry class). When I could finally see the board, I quickly crossed out the first name at eye level, Sgt. Eric Lloyd Kindig. Though I would eventually wind up sending cards to others too, I embarked on this first one with all the enthusiasm I usually reserved for theorems. It looked to me like romance was the real purpose of the project, and since I already had a boyfriend who was making my life miserable, there seemed no point in it. Besides, I couldn't believe Prince Charming would arrive wearing combat boots.

The reply came a month later—a fat, enticing envelope that perked up my interest by its sheer weight alone. The writer, I reasoned, was either literate or at least fancied that he was, which had a certain merit in and of itself. Standing over the heat register in the dining room, wearing the hideous blue-plaid uniform, I ripped the envelope open and read. After the usual "got your letter . . . thank you for writing . . . hearing from somebody back home made the holidays so much brighter" came pages of thoughtful prose, handwritten on both sides of five pieces of legal-size paper. Feelings about the war, descriptions of Vietnamese children, commentary on books he was reading, even a part about his girlfriend back home in Ohio segued neatly, paragraph after paragraph, into strong evidence that I'd finally uncovered a true romantic, a man with a heart. I looked up from the letter to my mother who was standing at the ironing board pressing one of my father's flannel shirts.

"Mom," I said, "I'm going to marry this guy."

She laughed.

Eric and I have been married for twenty-two intense years. We wrote for a year, lost touch for a few months, then finally met on January 17, 1970. For me, it was love at first sight; but he likes to say that he's the cautious type, so it took him an entire week to be sure. We became engaged three weeks after we met and were married four months after that. People called it a Cinderella story, and in many ways it was. He was six foot two and handsome; I was five foot two and weighed ninety pounds. He was twenty-six to my nineteen. After a storybook wedding in a grand cathedral and a romantic honeymoon to Virginia Beach, he whisked me off to an insignificant speck on the map thirty miles west of Akron. But the important part is, we were madly, passionately, deeply in love.

It could have been a disaster. It probably *should* have been one. Statistically, the odds of our marriage surviving were somewhere on par with the chance of discovering living beings on Mars. Aside from my youth and the difference in our ages, he was Protestant, I was Catholic; he voted Republican, I cast my lot with the Democrats; he grew up in a hand-hewn log cabin in the country, I was raised in a narrow old house in the inner city; his family looked like a Norman Rockwell painting, mine like a scene from Ellis Island. But more important, he was calm, logical, sane, and wise, and I was high-strung, emotional, neurotic, and smart. For the first seventeen years we flourished anyway, adopted two daughters from Korea, built a house and a business, and launched my career as a writer. And then, as abruptly as it had begun, the fairy tale ended.

SHATTERED ILLUSIONS

In 1989, Eric's business was embezzled by a person I'd warned him about, and we very nearly lost everything we'd built. For fifteen years I'd watched as he tolerated the flagrant abuse of time, money, and benefits by this person while making only the feeblest attempts to stop it. After the embezzlement I no longer saw Prince Charming when I looked at my husband. What I saw was a man who'd lacked the stamina to take a stand and put some muscle behind it—a man who hadn't protected his family. I was deeply disillusioned.

What I didn't realize then is that sooner or later most wives become disenchanted. Sometimes it's as sudden and dramatic as it was for me, but usually it's a slow, insidious process that leaves us wondering whatever happened to the shining promise of love. I've talked to women who blamed it on infidelity, alcoholism, financial disaster, and in-laws and to others who pointed the finger of blame at small breaches of trust—jokes told at their expense, husbands who took them for granted and didn't bother with the niceties anymore. All of these things are no doubt factors, but I've come to believe that the bottom-line reason for disenchantment is that we cling tenaciously to romantic myth in spite of growing evidence that the Cinderella story doesn't mirror reality in the nineties any more than it has at any other time in history.

After sloughing through the murky waters of disenchantment I have learned much—about myself, about marriage, and especially, about healing. I have also learned that Thomas Wolfe was right when he said you can never go home again. After making the journey back from disenchantment, I've found that it's impossible for a relationship to be the same as it was before. Eric and I—and other survivors who have shared their stories with me—have had to forge something different, something better. Although I think I'll always carry a sense of lost innocence, I know now that real intimacy begins only when we give up the idea that a husband should be a prince who will never let us down, a superhero who will protect us from unpleasant realities, and a magician who will fill up all the empty spaces inside.

Even when no sudden calamity shakes our foundations, the Cinderella myth is destructive because it keeps relationships from reaching their full potential. When we peer at each other through rose-colored glasses, use romantic gestures as the yardstick to measure the depth of love, and harbor impossible expectations, we practically guarantee disenchantment. When it comes, as it inevitably will, it brings feelings of hopelessness, betrayal, and anger. How we handle these feelings depends a lot on who we are, our belief systems, and how much we value the relationship.

I never questioned whether I wanted to stay married, but I knew that somehow I had to find joy in it again. In spite of the rage and the profound sense of betrayal I felt, I still believed that maybe it was even possible. Other women I talked with spoke of staying married but shutting down emotionally and using romantic fantasy to escape from the drabness of everyday life. Some talked of turning into critical, demanding shrews even as they loathed themselves for doing so, while still others spoke of anguish, betrayal, and the bone-deep conviction that the dream had slipped away forever. A few chose to begin the search for a new prince, one who would better live up to the romantic ideal. But we need only look at the statistics to see that almost one out of two marriages ends in divorce, and the success rate of second marriages is even more dismal than that of first marriages, to realize that most seekers come up empty.

Living as I have in the state of marriage for more than half my life, I had developed the idea that younger women approach relationships differently than I did. That's why the Prince Charming commercial brought me up short. In the nineties with a new millennium close at hand, even women in their thirties and forties don't appear to be as guileless as they once were about love and marriage. Unlike our predecessors, we've read the right books, programed our VCRs to record Oprah, Phil, and Sally, and successfully negotiated our way through the halls of independence. Chances are, we've also been disenchanted, perhaps more than once. Never would we be so naive as to believe that one mortal male could make our every dream come true! And yet, amazingly enough, that's exactly what many of us do believe.

Whether we're progressive or traditional, housewives or professionals, we all long for the same thing—a money-back guarantee that we'll live happily ever after as soon as we find the right prince. And it's precisely this deeply imbedded hope that causes us to don the spangled gown of the princess and abdicate the responsibility that would open the door to the equality and intimacy we seek. It makes us emotionally dependent and causes us to send confusing messages to the men who would be our princes, the men who have also fallen victim to the myth of Cinderella and Prince Charming.

So entwined are the roots of the myth in our cultural thinking that in the twentieth century alone romantic fantasy has survived five major wars, the Great Depression, the sixties, Reaganomics, and the massive redefinition of the American family. So inured have we become to it that we don't even notice the subtle, but skewed, messages about love slung at us daily by books, movies, song lyrics, and even ads for cars and blue jeans. No wonder Cinderella lurks beneath our sleek, well-crafted exteriors, and no wonder men say they're confused about what women want.

BEYOND A STORYBOOK LOVE

Traditionally, Prince Charming has been a superhero in an ermine-trimmed cape. He's strong, self-assured, dynamic, romantic, and invincible. He never forgets birthdays or anniversaries, knows what we want before we put it into words, and builds a wide, deep moat to keep unwelcome intruders from our door. If, by chance, he also happens to be handsome, successful, rich, and powerful, so much the better. The only problem is that today we want all this and more. Today we want Alan Alda in shining armor. Or at least we say we do. But the truth is, we're not always comfortable with men's feelings of inadequacy, fear, and anxiety, especially when those feelings threaten our own sense of security. Besides, even when we *didn't* want Alan Alda in shining armor, the Cinderella myth didn't work because it's based on the assumption of perfection. Also, it implies that the prince must be strong and the princess weak, which makes it difficult to form a union of two actualized adults.

About a year after the embezzlement, when we were finally beginning to walk the road to financial recovery, I began to realize the depth of my disenchantment. Before that we were too busy focusing on survival. But one Saturday morning I had coffee with my good friend Julie, and she said something that jolted me into the awareness that both she and I were unwitting victims of a myth I didn't even know I subscribed to.

"Eileen, it's funny, isn't it?" she said musingly, as we watched our youngest daughters playing outside the kitchen window in the piles of autumn leaves. "Here we are wearing the right clothes, spouting the right rhetoric, and underneath it all, we're no different than women have ever been. We're throwbacks to the Middle Ages."

"Throwbacks?" I asked the question, but a profound uneasiness told me I already knew the answer.

"Think about it. You feel betrayed because Eric made a mistake and didn't live up to his promise to keep you secure. And I'm no different. I can whine and moan and say how awful everything is, but Jim doesn't dare do the same. He's supposed to say everything's either okay or will be okay and then *fix it*, or I'm off the wall. We want somebody to protect us."

I couldn't argue that point. I'd never met a woman yet who didn't want to feel secure. But was that really so terrible?

"Let me tell you something," Julie continued. "When my mother was dying I handled everything: the hospital, the doctors, even the funeral decisions. But one night I was in the hospital elevator with my father, and all of a sudden he broke down and started sobbing. I'll never forget how I felt. It was like if my father was out of control then the world must be ending. I'm the same way with Jim. I want him to be vulnerable, but only as long as he's solid as a rock. And I want to be independent, but only as long as my backup system's in A-1 condition."

I knew she was right. I wanted the same thing. And I also wanted romance and passion and happily ever after. To sum it up, I wanted perfection from a human being!

When we respond to marriage as storybook characters we deprive each other of our own humanity. An old Greek adage says that people who eat bread and salt together forge bonds too great to be broken. Bread and salt are metaphors for the dailiness of human life, as well as for the joys and sorrows that mark, bless, elevate, and enlighten it. To enter a long-term union of hearts, minds, spirits, and flesh means sharing both the ordinary and the exalted in full celebration of who we are, with all our good and bad exposed. To do it successfully is to touch undiscovered parts of ourselves and to glimpse something far greater still—our relationship with the divine.

It's difficult enough to grow more intimate in our fast-paced, constantly changing world; trying to do it while acting out imaginary roles is ludicrous. Sooner or later, the magic dust settles at our feet, and we're left as I was—betrayed, hurt, and profoundly angry.

When I realized that behind the clothes and the rhetoric I was really a Cinderella after all, I began to do a little research into the Cinderella myth, and I discovered something very interesting. Cinderella is passive only in the American version of the tale. First, she docilely puts up with all that abuse from the wicked stepmother and the pair of nasty stepsisters, then doesn't even question her fairy godmother when the old woman turns up with the improbable idea of going to the ball in a souped-up pumpkin, wearing see-through shoes. *Then* she sits shivering in the cinders waiting for the prince to show up and rescue her. Finally, relieved to have somebody to take care of things, she asks nothing, just hands over her trust like a dowry and, with stars in her eyes, climbs up on the back of his white horse and canters naively off into the sunset.

In the European versions of the tale Cinderella at least shows some gumption. She takes responsibility for herself, trusts her own instincts, harbors no illusions, and still gets the man. I like that a lot. And I firmly believe that it's possible.

If we're ever to find a mature, mutually supportive, intimate union (and, conversely, know when we *don't* have one and aren't likely to achieve it in a given relationship), we have to realize that real life will never be an American fairy tale. There are no Cinderellas and no Prince Charmings—just real people who sometimes love magnificently, sometimes botch it badly, and usually over the course of a lifetime manage to do both. We have to realize that, like it or not, Cinderella has clay feet and the prince wears combat boots.

CHAPTER TWO

Happily Ever After?
Beyond Storybook Romance

Not long ago I received a letter from a bright, articulate single woman in her early thirties who posed a provocative question: Who would ever want to get tangled up with a man after facing how unfulfilling a relationship often is?

Knowing the price we pay for falling under the spell of romantic fantasy, it's easy to see where she's coming from. Journalists regale us almost daily with stories about the "second shift," reminding us of the dismal fact that women may have advanced professionally but we're still doing most of the housework and child rearing—and probably earning less money during the first shift than our husbands. Studies also show that married men live longer and healthier lives than their single counterparts, yet these same studies fail to assure married women of equally beneficial results. Government figures point to the grim increase in the number of homes headed by single mothers living in poverty, as well as to the trend for men to attain a higher standard of living following a divorce than their wives. And every day Ann Landers and Dear Abby respond to heartbreaking letters from women who have been cheated on, used, abused, ignored, and abandoned by the men who'd promised to love them forever.

Just this week I listened to one friend pour out the frustration of being married to a man whose needs must always come first, even when it comes to her career and the money she absolutely must earn to meet their monthly expenses. Another bemoaned the fact that her mate is gone five nights out of seven. Then on Saturday, my daughter was in a wedding where one of the young bridesmaids, the mother of two babies, had just discovered that her husband is having an affair. If marriage often leads to frustration, loneliness, and heartache, why bother? How can it be worth it? *Is* it worth it?

Even from the darkest depths of my own disenchantment, mine would have been the voice crying out in the wilderness, "Yes!" That's how much I believe in marriage. For me, the sadness of disenchantment sprang from the very fact that I had experienced so much love, trust, empathy, and growth over the course of my marriage that I was afraid I might never know these things again. Somehow, in spite of the rose-colored glasses I'd worn for so long, I'd managed to see clearly that pledging love and fidelity to one person for a lifetime can bring an intimacy no other relationship offers.

INTIMACY IN THE TRENCHES

Each stage of my children's development has been

a small miracle. But from the beginning I've known that my goal, bittersweet though it is, is to raise them to become independent adults who will leave home to pursue their own lives. Because marriage doesn't have separation as its goal, it gives us the time, space, and security to probe every facet of who we are, both as individuals and as a couple. In marriage, we mine the most elemental parts of ourselves: our sexuality, our spirituality, and our ability to love and to be loved.

Marriage offers more than a hand to hold through the milestone events of life: creating a home, raising children, pursuing our life's work, and growing old. While having someone with whom to share these accomplishments is ostensibly why we walk down the aisle, if marriage were an exotic cruise these happenings would represent only the most conventional ports of call. We wouldn't want to miss them, but neither would we feel we'd savored the full experience if we hadn't also escaped from the packaged itinerary to explore the nooks and crannies that don't show up in the tour guide. These side trips can make the difference between a good marriage and an intimate one.

Though Eric and I had fallen victim to a romantic illusion that could very well have destroyed our relationship, we'd made enough side trips for me to know that marriage could be the safest harbor we would ever discover. The knowledge that someone has pledged to love, cherish, and stick by us through thick and thin gives us the freedom and security to face, dissect, and assimilate the most puzzling and painful parts of our lives. Because of our marriage, I was finally able to come to terms with my tumultuous relationship with my family, and Eric was able to lay to rest his experiences in Vietnam.

A highly educated woman, whom I admire as much for her relationship with her husband as I do for her intelligence, told me that she, too, credits marriage with much of her personal growth. She and her husband have great fun together, share a lively interest in books and family life, and talk in depth about values and goals. But one of the most important lessons that intimacy has taught her is to meet pain head on and share it instead of retreating with it like a wounded animal.

"George and I have never lived an enchanted existence," she said. "So I guess I didn't have too many illusions. Almost from the beginning we had to face hard things. First we lost several babies, and then we had to deal with our daughter's serious health problem. Each time one of these things happened I wanted to go off by myself and hide, but my husband wouldn't let me. He drew me out and was there for me, helping me handle it. Because I never expected him to do that, I found it thrilling."

The word *thrilling* caught me by surprise. Thrilling is a word I associate with once-in-a-lifetime adventures and the kind of romance that makes your toes curl. And here was this thirty-something suburban woman with a doctorate in philosophy using it to describe how she felt about her husband supporting her through miscarriages and a child's hospitalization!

But intimacy isn't just about such weighty matters as birth and death, pain and fear. Sharing the seemingly inconsequential things that remind us we aren't slugging it out in life's trenches by ourselves is every bit as important. One evening I was at a meeting and saw a young wife flash a grin and a wink at her husband, not because anything of consequence was happening, but because they were in separate groups and she wanted to establish contact with him. When he winked back I couldn't help but smile and think to myself that we get married as much for those winks as we do for anything else.

When I was disenchanted it never occurred to me to worry that if a sudden crisis arose Eric and I wouldn't be there for each other. Our bond was strong enough that I knew we'd be magnetically drawn together if one of our children became ill or a relative died. What I saw slipping away, and wasn't so sure we could regain, were the small manifestations of intimacy that remind us of our link in the midst of children's needs, work responsibilities, social demands, and general chaos. Until they were absent from my life, I didn't realize that a great deal of the abiding fulfillment we find in marriage consists of private jokes, knowing glances, and being able to read each other's subtle signals.

A woman whose husband died suddenly told me that it's not so much the romance and passion she misses as it is setting the second place for dinner, arguing about politics, and snuggling up like "spoons" in bed. It's not that romance isn't important. It's just that romance is only one factor in a relationship that is infinitely more complex and creative than Cinderella and Prince Charming would have us believe.

THE GIFT OF MEANING

Shortly after Eric and I discovered that the business finances had been embezzled, I was forced to abandon my writing career (which was *finally* beginning to blossom) to work at a local nursing home. At first I was too numb and frightened about the future to focus on how bitterly I resented it. I was also trying to be supportive of Eric, who was as numb and frightened as I was. But after a while the bitterness crept in as surely and stealthily as a blanket of fog. I'd come home each evening after putting in twelve hours as director of admissions and community relations and fall into bed exhausted, certain that I could no longer endure another hopeless, miserable day. Then I'd look over at Eric sleeping and feel anger swell inside me like a tidal wave. *If you'd only listened when I tried to tell you . . .* I'd think.

How easy it would have been to just give up! I'd find my thoughts drifting to other people whose situations appeared so much easier than ours, and the anger would blacken until I'd end up doing the most dangerous thing we can do when trying to recover from disenchantment: fantasizing about starting over with someone new. Although I wasn't sure just who that new Prince Charming should be, I did know he had to be someone strong enough to keep preventable disaster from raining down on the heads of his family. Looking back, I can see that that line of thinking, coupled with the perilous vulnerability I wore at the time, could have been exploited by someone who was just as disenchanted as I was. And yet, I also know I would never have given up that easily. My relationship to Eric and our two children is what gives my life purpose. I *need* them to count on me, expect things from me, and care if I'm not there.

I don't mean to imply that the only path to fulfillment is marriage. Many women are happily and creatively single, living lives of service and substance often envied by those who languish in unfulfilling or miserable marriages. What I *am* saying is that, for me, marriage and motherhood are part of why I get out of bed in the morning. As I tried to formulate an answer to my single friend's question about whether or not marriage was worth getting tangled up in, I kept returning to the word *meaning*. I am more than a wife and a mother, but marriage gives my life form and shape so that it is easier to express the myriad other parts of who I am. Being confident of the love and support of someone who has committed his life to me makes it less frightening to take risks, try new things, and express the facets of myself that I've kept hidden.

Certainly it would be easier sometimes not to be burdened by the demands of marriage. I'd like to be able to make plans without having to consult Eric's travel schedule, eat popcorn for dinner if I feel like it, not have to worry about him when he's away, and not have to put up with his reluctance to share feelings and his chronic restlessness that wakes me up at least a half-dozen times each night. But unless we care deeply for someone other than ourselves, our lives become shallow and empty. There comes a point when gratifying our every whim becomes more of a prison than a panacea. Yet this is one thing the Cinderella myth fails to address. Romantic fantasy concerns itself so exclusively with what Prince Charming is supposed to be giving *us* that it fails to address what we're supposed to be giving in return.

When I mentioned this to a woman who has been disenchanted for most of the nine years of her marriage, she immediately flew on the defensive. "It sounds to me like you're saying we ought to make a beeline back to the fifties with 'the little woman' running around frantically doing the master's bidding," she scoffed. "Thanks, but no thanks!"

Though I was surprised by her vehemence, I could also understand it. When we feel like a doormat it's difficult to find joy and satisfaction in caring about someone else, in doing things that will please him, and in inconveniencing or burdening ourselves for his benefit. The view of the wife "doing the master's bidding" is every bit as lopsided as that of Prince Charming charging around on his white horse making everything wonderful.

Marriage is about reciprocity, about giving and taking. Just as there are some aspects of being married I find restrictive, I know that Eric could just as easily come up with a list of his own complaints. In a world perfectly suited to him, he'd never have to make dinner when I'm in a deadline crunch, put up with my craziness when I lose confidence in myself, or listen to me harp about how much fat and sodium he's consuming. But the world isn't perfect and neither are we, so we have no choice but to accept some things we don't like for the simple reason that the value of love outweighs the hassle.

When I was disenchanted, fantasy only deepened my discontent. Fortunately, when I'd start daydreaming about a fairy-tale-perfect life with a prince more deserving of the title, I'd occasionally have the good sense to remind myself that lying next to me in that king-sized bed was not just a man whose anemic approach to business problems had almost wiped us out, but a man with whom I had shared the most significant events of my life: The adoptions of our daughters from Korea, our month in Ireland, the two teenage foster children who'd come to live with us in the mid-seventies, our sponsorship of a family of eight Vietnamese refugees, restoring our house, all the jumbled holidays, the times he believed in me when I didn't. The images would tumble and change like the view in a kaleidoscope, reminding me what I would be losing if I didn't live up to the promise to love and cherish him all the days of my life.

Though I don't believe that shared history is reason enough to remain in a marriage, it's certainly a factor to be considered, especially when the good memories are more abundant than the bad. By reflecting on the meaning that marriage has given our lives, we shore up our resources to confront and deal with the issues that cause us the deepest pain. The hard times in marriage extract a huge emotional price from us, but reminding ourselves of the reasons we marry for life makes it a little easier to stay committed.

FOR BETTER OR FOR WORSE

Commitment is crucial on the journey back from disenchantment. Though *commitment* is not an especially popular word in modern times, it's an important one, because without it there's little to keep us believing in marriage once the lights go out and the music stops playing. Commitment must not be confused with obligation, however. Many people say they're committed to marriage, yet live in abject misery. That's because they're really committed to something different: their children, their religious beliefs, their self-image, their reputation, their lifestyle, or even the *idea* of marriage. To find the satisfaction we seek in a lifelong relationship we have to be committed to the *person* we chose to be our partner—the man who would be our prince. And that's what trips us up. Few of us have problems latching on to "happily ever after," but when "happily" disappears, the idea of commitment gets more than uncomfortable.

Madeleine L'Engle, an author who has written eloquently and honestly about marriage, once said something in a magazine interview that left an indelible impression on me. Every marriage, she said, goes through "divorce periods," times when a husband and wife look at each other through a dull gray fog and ask, "What am I wasting my life on this for?" These are the times when it seems that love has failed us miserably. Some of us walk out the front door and never come back. As I plowed through that long, dark year of disenchantment, struggling for understanding and renewal, I thought of L'Engle's statement often and found hope in it. One of the biggest lies the Cinderella myth promotes is that the journey of love is linear. We aren't prepared for the switchbacks that take us into the dark woods along the way.

Those of us who take commitment seriously repeat our wedding vows with the purest of intentions, not only because we're sure we'll live happily ever after, but because we genuinely believe that marriage is forever. Few brides walk down the aisle thinking their dreams of love will go up in flames. Even fewer carry the business card of the most ruthless divorce lawyer in town just in case marriage doesn't turn out to be the sweet deal they'd bargained for.

It's not that we've forgotten our coworker's messy divorce, the neighbors' shouting matches, and our parents' stony silences punctuated only by the sound of cutlery scraping across dinner plates. Of course we remember. But that's *them*, we tell ourselves, not us.

We're like Romeo and Juliet, Cathy and Heathcliffe, Jane and Mr. Rochester. *Our* love will be immortal.

Certainly we're not naive enough to believe that marriage is a bed of roses and the bad won't come flying in on the wings of the good. But we do have a tendency to romanticize struggle the same way we romanticize love! Books and movies glorify couples who endure wars, famine, poverty, plagues, even the death of children, and still emerge entwined in one another's arms. "As long as we have each other we can survive anything," they gush, wiping the sweat from their furrowed brows and gazing passionately into each other's pained eyes. Watching them, we sigh with satisfaction, relieved to know that, once again, it's all just a matter of finding Mr. Right. Is it any wonder that when the "divorce periods" come, as they inevitably do, we're so ill-equipped to handle them? Nobody told us that love would include boredom, disinterest, and sometimes even stabs of pure hatred.

Commitment is a frightening word because it implies the negative as well as the positive. During the "sexual revolution" we, as a society, made a bold attempt to turn our backs on it entirely. We told ourselves we were liberated enough to seek gratification on our own terms with no strings attached. But for all our political assertions and experimentation, we married in record numbers. According to the United States Census Bureau, we said "I do" at the rate of 8.5 percent per thousand population in 1960, and at the rate of 10.6 percent by 1980. Even amid a "revolution," we found that it's no more gratifying to live without any strings to bind us than it is to live in a fairy-tale world. Once the excitement, novelty, and heady sense of emancipation wore off we were left staring into a gaping black void.

To whom, we began to wonder, could we turn to assuage the ache of our loneliness? With whom did we dare be totally vulnerable when we woke up scared in the middle of the night? Who cared enough to understand and rejoice with us in our successes? And who would be constant and dependable as we coped with continuous change in our lives and in the world? Instead of expecting to get some of our needs met by a human being who is as flawed as we are, we did a one-hundred-eighty degree turn and, like our predecessors, went in search of the mythical Prince Charming.

Difficult though it is, commitment tests our mettle. Anyone can stay in a relationship replete with fairy-tale trappings. But in admitting to and conquering disenchantment, we discover the depth of our own strength, build trust in our partner and ourselves, and embark on one of life's greatest adventures. Those who keep starting over, hopping from relationship to relationship, never explore the outer limits of intimacy.

Years ago I accompanied Eric to Oklahoma on a business trip where we met a fascinating couple. He was the curator of a museum; she a freelance writer specializing in history. One evening they took us out for a Chinese dinner and afterward back to their charmingly cluttered home where books, maps, and papers mingled happily with the dog, the cat, and the antique furniture.

We had been married only two years at the time; Les and Marilee were about to celebrate their twentieth anniversary. Although I remember being properly awed by their considerable professional achievements, today I'd be hard-pressed to list what those accomplishments were. What I remember most clearly about them is how obviously delighted they were with one another. They laughed at each other's witticisms, encouraged each other to talk about their work, ran and fetched each other coffee, and exchanged glances when they thought no one was looking. The current that jumped back and forth between them was enough to power a light bulb, but I, quite frankly, didn't know what to make of it. Because I was an unwitting, but fervent, subscriber to the Cinderella myth, I assumed that the early years of marriage when romance is at its peak are the best.

"Let's never be oldly-weds," I'd say to Eric whenever we'd see a middle-aged pair at a restaurant exchanging not more than three words from soup to dessert. From my perspective most long-term marriages were boring at best. But here was a couple who'd been together what seemed to me like *forever*, and suddenly I was wishing the years could fly by so Eric and I would reach this magic pinnacle, too! As a young, inexperienced Cinderella, I assumed that their happiness was the result of a closeness that had transformed them into a single entity—LesandMarilee rather than Les and Marilee.

Only now, on this side of disenchantment, can I replay that evening and see that what I responded to so positively was the reality of two distinct, separate individuals who lived fulfilling lives apart from one another, coming together for mutual support and pleasure. I had been offered an early, powerful glimpse of an important truth: *The goal of marriage is not to swallow up one's partner.* If only I'd been mature enough to understand.

TOGETHER ALONE

Midway through my period of disenchantment, Eric and I took the kids for a long weekend to Marietta, Ohio, an historic city located where the Ohio and Muskingum Rivers meet. Though I was looking forward to the respite—our first since the embezzlement a year and a half before—I harbored no expectations. We stayed at a lovely historic hotel, took a riverboat ride down the Ohio, scoured the antique shops, attended a melodrama aboard the *Becky Thatcher*, and did all the other "touristy" things people do on vacation. It was fun, but I felt detached, as though I were a single balloon floating alongside the bunch.

On our last day there we woke up early and walked in the golden light of a morning so still and sharp the birds sang grace notes and we responded in whispers. Except for a few pleasure boats and an occasional pedestrian, we had the world to ourselves. We decided to cross the Muskingum and soon came to an old wooden footbridge. Eric strode across first, with Caitie, our youngest, dancing alongside him, and Moira and me following. The ancient boards creaked; the gray waters of the river showed through the slats. Beside me, Moira begin to stiffen just before she froze about a third of the way across.

"I'm scared. I can't do it. It's too high and rickety."

"Sure you can!" Eric called. "Just look at me and keep walking." Slowly, he came toward us, urging her on with the sound of his voice.

Suddenly it was 1957 and I was six years old, standing at one end of the old Bowery Street bridge in Akron with my Irish grandmother on the other, coaxing me in her gentle brogue to pick my way across the rotting gray boards spanning the canal.

"You were afraid too," Eric said when we'd safely reached the other side.

I nodded. Moira's reluctance had dredged up a long-forgotten terror.

"Well, don't worry," he said. "I'll never leave you stranded."

Though his words were light and referred to nothing more than actual bridges of concrete and wood, my heart did a crazy little leap, and I felt almost giddy with a ridiculous glee.

"I know you won't," I replied just as lightly. "What do you say we have ice cream?"

"For *breakfast*?" Caitie asked, incredulous.

"Why not?"

By the time we packed the car and checked out of the hotel the giddiness was gone and I could feel the dread of returning to "the real world" begin to wash over me. Nothing had fundamentally changed, except one thing: I knew why I kept trying to cross the river. Even when the bridge is old and high and has scary spaces between the slats, there's somebody waiting for me on the other side.

That reminder gave me some balance and determination for the long, frightening journey that was far from complete. One day I would walk closely with my husband on a new, sunlit path. But first I had to learn to stand on that shaky bridge between us — alone.

CHAPTER THREE

The Princess Stands Alone
The Power of Self-Responsibility

It was shortly after nine p.m. and I was in my office, staring out the window at the snow dancing under the mercury lights.

Everything was done by then—all the paperwork filled in, signed, copied, filed, and faxed. I knew I should get home, but at that moment the nursing home seemed like the safest place in the world to be. Tomorrow I would have surgery to remove an ovarian cyst.

As could be expected, Eric was approaching the surgery in his usual calm, matter-of-fact way. Part of me was relieved, but another part was resentful that he wasn't more into the drama of the thing. He'd called earlier to say he'd made spaghetti for the kids and was watching a documentary on PBS. That's when I should have gone home, but I'd felt strangely compelled to have everything finished, including a list of instructions for Linda, who would be taking over my job until I got back.

My gaze fell on a slip of pink paper tucked under the jar of blue mints that always sat on the corner of my desk. It turned out to be two slips—one from Linda, the other from my boss, Gloria.

"Just wanted to let you know I'll be thinking about you tomorrow. You're in my prayers. Good luck! Love, Linda."

"Eileen, I know this is hard for you, but you'll do fine. I'll be there as soon as it's over. Much love, Gloria."

Up to this point I hadn't allowed myself to cry, but those notes did it. Instantly I was weeping—for myself, for Eric, for all the heartache of the past year and a half, for fear and old age and bad ovaries and whirling snow and notes on pink paper. *Well, kid, you're really on your own with this one,* a voice in my head said. *Nobody can get you through but you. Even Eric can't fix it.*

The thought brought me up short. I stopped crying and sat perfectly still, trying to comprehend the vastness of alone. It occurred to me that it had been a long time since I'd allowed myself to contemplate the fact that there are certain things every human being has to do for herself. No one, no matter how great his love, can endure our pain, wrestle our demons, live with our memories, or die our death.

Fortunately, I'm not an existentialist. I don't believe we're isolated beings fighting for survival in a purposeless universe. I believe there's a "season for all things under heaven." A season—and also a reason. I wasn't sure why I had to face this surgery when I already felt overwhelmed by the embezzlement, my disenchantment, and the alien world of the nursing home. But whatever the reason, I dug deep that night to find the faith that told me it was all for a greater good.

The next morning found me at the outpatient surgery by seven, gowned in drab blue cotton, lying in a pink vinyl recliner, hooked up to an IV. It took an interminably long time to get started, so Eric and I talked, made jokes, and didn't look at each other much. When it finally came time to begin, I stood up, dragging the IV pole, gave him a kiss (*the last one? a crazy voice asked*), and walked into the operating room. Shiny—high-tech. Scary.

Heart thundering in my ears, I lay down on the table. "I feel like the sacrifice," I joked. Everybody laughed.

Then I woke up. Machines beeping. Oxygen in my nose. Pain, incredible pain. If this was "belly button surgery," I'd hate to feel the real thing. Gingerly I slipped my hand beneath the sheet to feel the incision—and set off an alarm.

"No, no, you can't do that!" a nurse cried, rushing in behind the curtain.

"It hurts," I said. "A lot."

The anesthesiologist came over then. "You have a four-inch incision," he explained. "The cyst turned out to be bigger than they thought. Everything's okay, but we're going to have to transfer you to the hospital for four days."

"No!" At that I managed to sit bolt upright. "No hospital. I'm fine. I really am." I smiled to prove it.

He grinned back. "Well, lie down awhile and we'll see. Right now there's somebody out here waiting to see you."

Eric came in then, smiling. "Hi, Goose," he said softly.

"Hi." I reached for his outstretched hand, and

we both laughed nervously. Nothing in our two decades together had prepared us for this high-tech wonderland of stainless steel and people in shower caps. "Make them let me out of here, okay?"

He nodded. "I'll try."

"I know you will," I said, and it was true. Somehow, if it was possible, Eric would do it.

How we managed to pull it off, I don't know, because every medical person I've told this story to is aghast. But five hours later we were on the road toward home with my gynecologist's blessing. Apparently the fact that I'd been able to walk, continue a steady stream of upbeat patter, and keep from throwing up was enough to convince her it was safe to send me off in the care of a man who hyperventilates if one of the kids gets the stomach flu. She made a wise decision.

Coming home was a gift. Although the first night was rough, I was almost giddy with a sensation of strength and well-being. For eight hours I was sick to my stomach, but Eric cared for me with incredible tenderness. Over and over I kept saying, "It's like a miracle," because that's how it felt—miraculous to be home feeling so loved and cared for, to connect again with my husband after all those months of estrangement. Eric and I needed the four weeks of my recuperation to sort through what had happened to us in the past year. The whole experience proved to me that there is indeed a "season for all things under heaven."

EQUAL PARTNERS

Realizing that there are some things Eric cannot do for me forced me to shore up strength I didn't know I had and gave me insight into both marriage and the Cinderella myth. Surgery became a metaphor for the curious puzzle of marriage that asks us to be both strong and weak, alone and together.

When we become Cinderellas we abdicate responsibility for ourselves. Because the myth is predicated on the concept of the strong prince and the weak princess, it teaches us to enter romantic relationships crying, "Help me, save me, I can't make it without you!" when we should be saying, "You have strengths and weaknesses, and so do I. Let's help each other." Not surprisingly, we come to view the prince as a savior who has the power to make us ecstatically happy or hopelessly miserable and to protect us (if only he will) from every imaginable loss.

Rationally, most of us would agree that it's ridiculous to put such demands on a partner. But so deeply ingrained is the Cinderella myth in our psyches, that even while we're busy convincing ourselves that we're far too sophisticated to give it credence, it's hard at work shaping our expectations of marriage! Certainly for me to have some negative feelings about the embezzlement, and even about Eric's refusal to control the situation that led to it, is natural. But the root cause of my anger had as much to do with protection issues as it did with financial hardship. The bottom line was, I wanted safety from the arrows of life because I wasn't convinced I was capable of handling them.

Psychologist Lillian Rubin touches on this issue in her book *Intimate Strangers, Men And Women Together* (Harper and Row, 1983), when she relates her own deeply buried feelings about being "taken care of." Some years after she had become successful enough to shoulder her family's entire financial responsibilities, she and her husband decided that he would quit his job to pursue his interest in writing, with the understanding that he probably would be earning little or no money for a while. The decision was reached only after much discussion and mutual agreement, and Rubin felt certain it would work well. Much to her surprise, it didn't—at least not at first. Though she had never thought of herself as a Cinderella, she soon began to realize that she hated and even resented working because she *had* to, even though she loved her work. She wanted to know that if it ever became too burdensome she could quit and that her husband would provide her with a safety net.

There's nothing wrong with safety nets—as long as we provide them for each other. Where safety nets become a problem is when one person (Cinderella) becomes so needy that the other person (Prince Charming) is forced to become a live-in parent. The reason we marry is to live intimately with another human being. But as Stephanie Covington and Liana Beckett point out in their book *Leaving the Enchanted Forest: The Path from Relationship Addiction to Intimacy* (Harper and Row, 1988), we cannot find true intimacy as long as our relationships are unbalanced. When Cinderella is cast in the role of needy child and Prince Charming as benevolent father, equality doesn't stand a chance. Covington and Beckett also point out that parents and children can be close, but never intimate, for the simple reason that the child is dependent on the parent for basic survival. In order to function as an adult in a romantic relationship, we need to know that, if we had to, we could survive without it.

In some ways this was tough stuff to learn at almost forty. But, mercifully, my encounter with surgery also taught me another gentler lesson. It showed me that even though marriage is a grownup activity, there's still room within it to contain the child who lives inside each of us.

This past summer I was reminded of that truth once again as my friend Julie faced her father's slow, agonizing descent into death. By June, the spreading cancer that had begun in his bladder had confined him to bed and to the care of his children, who took turns staying with him in their childhood home a month at a time. June was Julie's month. Sometimes while he dozed restlessly she'd call me from Akron.

"I just thought of something today," she said once, her voice catching. "As soon as he's gone I'll never be anybody's little girl again."

Though I wanted to say it wasn't so, I couldn't because she was right and we both knew it. I was powerless to do anything but listen, care, be there. But slowly, as the long days wore on, her husband Jim discovered something he could do and did it without question. He granted her the freedom to be weak, needy, dependent, irrational, angry, selfish, weepy—in other words, to be childlike in her grief. It turned out to be the gift of healing. By the time her father died in October, Julie was strong, able to let go of the past, and function as an adult again.

For a husband and wife to parent each other, allow each other such periods of frailty, is beautiful, creative, and nurturing. It only runs aground when the arrangement becomes permanent. Ideally, we should take care of *each other*, protect each other when we can, and support each other through the pain we cannot or perhaps *should* not prevent. If couples are to survive disenchantment and enjoy intimacy, each partner has to take responsibility for his or her own emotional well-being.

When we marry, we can fall in love with the notion of joining so intensely with our partner that we become a single entity. While I still cherish the idea of the whole being greater than the sum of its parts, and believe good marriages should embody this characteristic of oneness, it concerns me that society encourages women to identify so intensely with romantic relationships that we forget where our partner leaves off and we begin. The other evening I heard a character in a situation comedy quip, "I don't have an identity anymore—I have a boyfriend." The reason we laugh at lines like this is because they smack of the truth.

It's tough to forge our own identities in marriage. Closing the educational gap that widened between the genders during the 1950s has certainly helped, as has our growing ability to be financially self-supporting. But until I experienced disenchantment for myself, I didn't understand that healthy autonomy in a relationship is impossible if we're short on self-esteem.

HOW DO I LOVE ME?

This book isn't meant to be a guide on how to raise self-esteem. There are already many such books on the market. But no discussion of disenchantment would be complete without examining the role self-esteem plays in romantic love. Strangely enough, I continue to learn powerful lessons about this from my seventeen-year-old daughter Moira.

One Sunday, a few weeks ago, she was sitting in the rocking chair in the family room watching television while I was making dinner. Her boyfriend was due any minute to spend the evening, and she was making no effort to change out of the jeans and oversized T-shirt she'd been wearing all day.

"Hadn't you better put some makeup on and get ready?" I called from the kitchen. Her refusal to look her best (unless the spirit moved her) had become a constant issue between us, one I couldn't seem to let go of.

"Oh, Mom!" Disgusted, she stalked into the kitchen, swinging her straight, waist-length black hair. "Why do you *do* this? I've told you a million times that he likes me the way I am. If he ever doesn't, then that's too bad for him."

"Okay. Whatever," I snapped, and began chopping onions with a vengeance. "It just seems to me that you'd want to look nice, that's all. All the other girls are dressed, curled, painted, perfumed, and trussed like turkeys!"

At that she laughed. "Mom, I weigh a hundred and five, remember?"

"I know, but you get my point."

"Yeah, and you get mine. I'd rather think about stuff that matters." The front of her T-shirt was printed with a slice of tropical rain forest and emblazoned with the words "Care About Tomorrow."

She drifted back to the family room and plopped down in the rocking chair, leaving me with a jumble of feelings that needed to be sorted out. Obviously, this issue wasn't entirely about lipstick. Or about Moira. It was about me, some old business from the past that I hadn't resolved. Secretly I was rather proud to have raised such an autonomous, free-spirited daughter (and a bit amazed that I *had*!). But I was also deeply afraid—afraid that she wouldn't be able to "compete" in the Prince Charming sweepstakes, that she'd lose her chance at happiness.

The more I struggle with this issue the clearer it becomes. Deep down I'm like most women, not entirely convinced that I'm okay the way I am. So if I look good and a man notices that, then (whew!) everything must be okay. Admittedly, makeup is an inconsequential issue, and I'm not saying we have to toss out our mascara wands along with the magic wand of romantic fantasy. I bring it up because it seems to embody the whole issue of self-esteem in microcosm. When we don't feel good about ourselves we come to romantic love as bottomless wells of neediness. *Fill me up, tell me everything's okay, tell me I'm okay. Be there for me!*

With this attitude we become hypersensitive. We're like radar detectors zooming in on every slight, every nuance of our partner's behavior. If he's preoccupied with work, he's "ignoring" us. If he answers curtly, he's mad at us—never mind that the computer's jammed and he has a report due at eight the next morning!

I have an unmarried friend who's intelligent, capable, and successful in her career, but who spends most of her life vacillating wildly between ecstasy and depression, depending on the whim of her current boyfriend. If he spends a lot of time with her, showers her with compliments, and builds her up emotionally, she's practically in orbit. If he doesn't, she can barely drag herself out of bed in the morning. But because she's a nineties kind of woman, Grace would never cling, cry, or beg for affirmation. When her needs go unmet, she either makes herself suddenly unavailable or else treats him with such coolness that he's soon jumping through hoops to win back her favor. On the surface, she appears totally in control, a really "together" kind of woman, but nothing could be further from the truth. She plays the same old game women have always played—she's just using updated rules.

Grace knows her behavior is dishonest and destructive and that as long as she engages in it she'll never have a fulfilling adult relationship. Sooner or later this relationship will leave her as profoundly disenchanted as all the previous ones. Either she'll decide that he's as disappointing as all the princes who have preceded him, or he'll get tired of jumping through hoops. Either way, it's not destined for success.

The reality of our aloneness and self-responsibility can be deeply frightening to encounter, and most of us (men included) spend an inordinate amount of time trying *not* to encounter it. But accepting this reality is essential to the journey back from disenchantment. By knowing in our hearts and souls that our sense of inner peace, self-worth, and well-being are no one's responsibility but our own, we bring to marriage a new depth and a realistic direction. A century ago, German poet Rainer Maria Rilke said it well: "Love consists in this, that two solitudes protect and touch and greet each other." The operative word is, and always will be, *solitudes*.

This has been one of the hardest lessons for me to learn, but I believe it saved our marriage. As I took more responsibility for myself and embraced the limitations of even the best kind of human love, I realized that wholeness could be mine—but not because of my connection to a man. Wholeness would come as I continued to grow up—not only emotionally, but spiritually as well.

CHAPTER FOUR

Prince Charming in the Sky
The Gifts of Mature Spirituality

It was a red-gold day, brilliant sun spiking through trees on fire. In my head a prayer, a plea, an incantation, rattled around like a loose marble, *OhmyGodOhmyGodOhmyGod.*

I followed the gray string of sidewalk intently, as though it might lead me somewhere, anywhere, away from the truth we'd heard last night.

"There's no question your funds have been embezzled," our accountant told us. "But it's worse than that, I'm afraid. The taxes haven't been paid, either. You owe a whopping bill to the IRS. I don't think you have any choice but to sell."

"*No!*" Eric's face had been white as chalk dust, mine no doubt a mirror, but the word had burst out of us both in unison. I'd get a job, we'd both get jobs, anything to save the business, anything. . . . Now here I was walking down East Liberty Street past houses with swags of Indian corn hanging off front doors that opened, surely, into worlds untouched by calamity.

I suppose I thought of myself as a religious person then, more or less so, anyway. I went to church services on Sundays, so it wasn't entirely out of character for me to be invoking God's name in a moment of terror and despair. I paced myself to the rhythmic "OhmyGods" in my head, and it helped. Calmer, calmer.

Yes, I would get a job. But where? I hadn't worked in fifteen years. Before we'd adopted our kids I'd been a newspaper reporter—first for a small weekly, later for a mid-sized daily—but I seriously doubted I could keep up with the pace of a computerized newsroom even if somebody did hire me. What else could I do? Uh . . . nothing.

Apply for the job at the nursing home, a voice that sounded like mine said in my head. It was so clear, certain, and directive that for a second it stunned me into something resembling normalcy. But then I came to my senses and figured I was surely going crazy. The ad in the newspaper had listed at least five qualifications, and I didn't have one of them. But the voice wouldn't be quelled that easily: *Do it. It's yours.*

It took me a week to muster the courage, but finally I sent in a résumé, which except for my freelance writing credits was a privileged woman's laundry list of benevolent causes. I was called in for an interview three days later, and I got the job the day after that. What's more, the salary was the exact figure I'd calculated we needed.

At this point, disenchantment was still a foreign country I wouldn't visit for another six months. But the voice in my head telling me to apply for the job would ultimately prove to be the greatest guide on the journey back. That voice was not only the sound of my own intuition, but more important, a call to travel the spiritual path.

WAKING UP TO A SPIRITUAL REALITY

"Do you believe that having a lot of faith makes you a stronger person and helps you in your relationships?" Julie asked me the other day. "It looks to me like a lot of these religious types just latch on to God like a life preserver."

My answer surprised her because I had never been one to speak of spirituality in terms of absolutes. "Yes," I said without a moment's hesitation, "definitely I believe it."

According to *Newsweek* magazine, 57 percent of Americans—some forty-three million people—attend a church or synagogue. Over 80 percent of baby boomers consider themselves religious and claim they believe in life after death, even though two-thirds of them have stopped attending church at one time or another. Among those who return to organized religion, the most common reason cited for doing so is the desire to discover the meaning of life.

These figures are significant, not so much because they indicate a rise in church attendance, but because they tell us how universal the spiritual quest is. As we begin to realize that our need for fulfillment and purpose cannot be met by material things, career success, *or even by our most significant relationships*, we hear the murmuring of the heart that naturally reaches beyond the limits of the material world to explore the mystery of things unseen. We begin to be open to faith.

Going through religious motions, such as attending church services, is so different from being spiritually awake and in tune. By the time Julie posed her question I had a much clearer understanding of what she meant when she said that so many religious people seem anything but strong and serene. As I began to make the connection between romantic myth and my own neediness, I realized one major reason we become Cinderellas: We lack an essential trust, both in ourselves and in a being greater than ourselves who sustains and empowers us.

Too often, spiritually as well as politically, we spout all the right rhetoric and perform all the right rituals, but essentially we remain needy children, looking for someone to re-parent the parts of us that weren't well parented in childhood. Instead of turning to religion as a source of genuine security and empowerment, we turn to it for protection from reality. Conditioned as we are to expect someone (Prince Charming) or something (romance) to fill the gaping holes in our hearts, it's little wonder so many of us welcome God into our lives in much the same way we welcome a mate. God becomes a sort of Prince Charming in the sky, a masterful, omnipotent (if somewhat capricious) father who has the power to make us magically and ecstatically happy if only we'd do the right things.

"I'm mad at God," my friend Grace told me over lunch one day. It wasn't the first time I'd heard her say it, but I'd never paid much attention, as she'd always laughed as though it were the punch line of a self-deprecating joke.

Grace is the intelligent, capable woman with the good job who looks to her relationships with men to define how she feels. The reason she's so angry is because six years ago she married a man with whom she was deeply in love. Because he was a devout Roman Catholic, she converted to his faith and soon became as committed to it as he was. Before the wedding she and Jack mutually agreed that the cornerstone of their relationship would be their faith in God. Almost immediately the new marriage ran into trouble. Despite counseling, it ended in an ugly, scarring divorce after only a few turbulent years.

"We prayed together, were involved in church activities, did all the right things, but it still didn't make a difference," she said bitterly. "Now I feel doubly betrayed—by Jack and by God." Grace knows that by remaining in her present destructive relationship she's courting disaster again, but she's too bereft to end it. She simply doesn't believe anymore that she has any control over what happens in her life.

When I finally heard what my friend was saying, I took a harder look at what I expected God to do for me. Did I view him as a celestial vending machine, eating my quarters or dispensing licorice when I punched the button for Sweet Tarts?

Certainly Grace was revealing her profound sorrow over the loss of her dreams for a happy, long-lasting marriage, but her feelings went far deeper than that. She was also mourning the loss of a spirituality that had seemed sustaining, but had turned out to be just as ephemeral as romantic love. Grace was disenchanted with God!

FINDING GOD IN A GROWN-UP WORLD

Many people, including psychologists, would argue that religion is a crutch, a childish knee-jerk response to pain by people who lack the inner strength to function in the real world. I disagree. Just as I don't believe that romantic love is childish, I don't believe that true spirituality is based on infantile needs. What happened to Grace is precisely what happens to any of us when we succumb to the false promise of romantic myth in our relationships. She came to God with lofty, oversimplified expectations and was devastated to learn that faith, like love, requires responsibility without a money-back guarantee of protection from pain.

Like so many of us, Grace viewed religion as a safety net. As long as she performed its rituals and chanted its incantations, she thought she could be assured that things would go well for her. When God didn't live up to her expectations, becoming disenchanted was a natural reaction for her. As her belief wobbled on its cracked foundation, she threw herself into a new relationship, more needy than ever, more desperate for it to fill her up, give her happiness, or at the very least, take away the chronic debilitating pain.

Because she no longer believes in hope, peace, guidance, solace, and rejuvenation—the very things in which we must trust if we're ever to abandon our Cinderella selves and become responsible adult partners in our relationships—it makes no difference whether or not this relationship is good for her in the long run. All she's interested in is feeling good *now*.

As we venture along the spiritual path, it's tempting to do exactly what Grace did and create a Prince Charming of our own in the sky who will magically protect us from pain as long as we "do the right things." It's comforting to believe that if we can't count on protection in the physical world, we can at least take refuge in the spiritual! The problem is, spirituality is both more difficult and more liberating than that. It requires us to take responsibility, make choices for ourselves, and trust our own journey, the hardest things of all to do for those of us who have always looked outside ourselves for happiness.

In my own way, I, too, had created a Prince Charming in the sky. Until I was faced with near calamity and disenchantment, prayer for me was something either done on Sunday as part of a familiar liturgy that appealed to me on an aesthetic level or else a pleading, begging monologue in times of distress—OhmyGodOhmyGodOhmyGod. I now know that faith and frightened pleading are worlds apart. To forge a trusting union with either God or a mate we can't cower in the corner and beg for protection. We have to be willing to see ourselves as we really are, recognize risk, and open our hearts anyway. What frightens and upsets the Cinderella inside us is that living the spiritual life doesn't insulate us from pain or from groping in the wilderness. At times we will hurt, and we will feel lost. We can count on it. We can count on it in marriage, too.

It's impossible to close the book on Cinderella and Prince Charming without first discovering a place inside ourselves where a deep sense of knowing resides. Until the embezzlement, I didn't know how strong I could be or that a hero is not always perfect. I certainly didn't know I could survive life outside the fairy tale. But in making these discoveries, I learned that I could trust myself to recover from pain as well as to trust that even the most difficult legs of my journey would lead me exactly where I needed to go. I began to trust that I was being guided by someone outside myself and all was well.

Insights didn't come in great lightning-bolt bursts, however. They came quietly, often not revealing their meaning, but forcing me to think about them over a period of time until at last a dim light gleamed in the distance.

One evening during my season of disenchantment, I stood at the back door of our family room gazing out at the sun setting over the lake behind our house. Through the darkening pines the sky was streaked red, orange, and violet. Two people in a canoe glided silently across the shimmering water, and as I watched them, tears began to well up in my eyes. *How beautiful,* I thought. *How amazing.* I felt such a poignant tenderness, an almost mystical oneness with life around me—with the trees, the water, the sky, and the two people in the canoe. Though I couldn't have put it into words at the time, I sensed that it had something to do with trust, a trust that there is order and constancy in life and the universe, even when appearances would tell us otherwise. Only much later did I realize that I was part of this order and constancy, that I, too, was where I belonged in the universe and would be empowered to endure well and strong.

I don't believe it's necessary to practice the rituals of religion to feel as I did at the back door that evening. That incredible leap of the heart is simply *there*, prompted by the spectacle of a starry sky, moments of creative passion, a mere glimpse of the divine light I can only call grace. Our relationship with the mystery of God and life around us is elemental. Learning to trust that relationship makes it possible to risk. As we search for a deeper understanding of God and our spiritual nature, we can't help but begin to discover who we really are and to find meaning in our own journey, too.

Ever since the embezzlement, I had felt a strong

pull toward introspection. Tears, once rare, lay right at the surface. More and more often I was drawn to books of a spiritual nature, to writing in my journal, to contemplation. Though I didn't realize it when it began, this process of spiritual awakening was the beginning of the abandonment of my Cinderella self, the start of deep healing. Later, as I came to understand the correlation between spiritual and personal growth and the ability to discard romantic fantasy, I began, tentatively, to talk about it with other women. The fact that I found a few who had already made this discovery for themselves buoyed my belief.

"I've discovered such unbelievable peace," a woman named Barbara said quietly. "Before I became more spiritually whole I was never satisfied. Oh, there were periods of satisfaction, I suppose, in the early months of marriage and right after the baby was born, but it didn't last. I was so demanding and critical. I wanted my husband to make me happy and fill up all the empty places inside me, and he couldn't do it. Now that I've stopped trying to make that happen, he's beginning to fill more of them. Does that make any sense?"

Yes, it makes much sense. When we meet each other without huge, overwhelming demands, we're freer to give and take because it is right and natural, not because we're compelled. Learning to trust our relationship with God is the first step toward coming to peace with ourselves and flowing with the realities of life.

Most women who struggle with disenchantment in their relationships feel emotionally impoverished in some way. They talk of parents who were abusive, cold, demanding, critical, insensitive, withdrawn, controlling, or smothering. They've learned not to trust their own instincts and resources. In their book *Trusting Ourselves* (Atlantic Monthly Press, 1990), Drs. Karen Johnson and Tom Ferguson make the important point that the healthier her family of origin, the easier it is for a woman to trust herself. They also identify five fathering styles that cause problems in this area of daughters' development: the White Knight, who makes his daughter his little princess; Big Daddy, who solves all problems; Pygmalion, whose daughter forever remains his pupil, never his equal; the Patriarch, who is uncomfortable with feelings and will step into the family foray only to settle disputes or assert his authority; and the Invisible Man, who is either physically or emotionally absent.

As women living in a world that continues to denigrate female strength and accomplishment, it's virtually impossible to escape totally the feeling that we're genetically weak and emotionally ineffectual, even if we were raised by parents who worked overtime to build our self-esteem. It's little wonder then that those raised in homes where parents imparted negative messages about trust find it so difficult to believe deeply in themselves—or in God. But the good news is, we are all spiritual beings, and when we are ready to recognize God's presence in our lives, he will meet us right in the midst of reality.

MAKING ROOM FOR GOD

At the first stirring of real spirituality in me, I knew I needed to find space in my life and heart for a deeper relationship with God. I began to set aside a time every day for quiet reading, prayer, writing in my journal, and most important, silence. Those who know me well would no doubt be amused by the latter, as I have never by nature been a quiet person. Eric has always said that I have two speeds—fast and faster. I talk constantly, fly around like a windup toy, and work on sixteen things at once. To function even for a short while without perpetual motion was a challenge, one that proved steadily difficult. Reading and writing came naturally. Praying wasn't so hard either, because praying meant talking and, God knows, I was good at that! What was hard was sitting in quiet contemplation, turning off the constant buzz of thoughts and ideas in my overactive brain, and simply listening in silence.

Sometimes during these sessions I would feel nothing, not even a merciful release from the worry and problems that seemed my constant companions. I would wonder whether the whole exercise wasn't just a waste of time or yet one more romantic notion. At those times God seemed very far away, and I, extremely weak and doubting. But other times a gathering strength would roll like thunder within me, and once again I'd catch hold of belief. On a few occasions I was rewarded by a feeling of both profound calm and heightened awareness, and I would hear the voice of intuition or feel a sense of positive direction.

Of course coming to silence as a form of prayer and self-understanding is not well understood in American culture. We thrive on noise! Even when we make a phone call and it's placed "on hold" or take a quick trip in an elevator, we can count on Muzak for distraction. God forbid that we should ever have to listen to our own inner voice, that we should be alone with our pain and fear! Even when our children attempt to retreat in solitude we want to draw them out, tell them to "snap out of it," give them something to do. Is it any wonder that we grow up not knowing how to be alone? What's sad is that this fear of solitude and silence serves only to fuel the Cinderella myth, because it keeps us frantically seeking external gratification instead of drawing on personal and spiritual power.

While I can't overstress the importance of silence in the quest to know both God and ourselves, I also strongly recommend journal writing, which is nothing more than bearing written witness of our spiritual journey. Ever since I was about ten and received my first diary—one of those gold-edged, vinyl-covered little books that comes complete with its own tiny key—I have been fascinated by the idea of bearing witness. But like so many people, I'd find myself writing for an audience (usually posterity!), becoming bored by what seemed a very mundane life, or feeling acutely embarrassed by what I'd written once the intensity of the moment had passed. And so I'd give up and not write for long periods. It wasn't until I began to write my way through disenchantment that I finally understood these important truths: the only audience that matters is ourselves, a journal is not a spine-tingling retelling of external events, and all feelings are valid even after they've drifted away!

Journal writing is a spiritual discipline that furthers our growth, not only because it enables us to look within, but because of its dailiness. Doing this basic task every day even when we're too tired or too busy becomes, in its way, a form of prayer that strengthens and sustains us at our core.

I think of the words of a friend when I suggested she might benefit from this kind of journey of the heart. "You've got to be kidding!" she exclaimed. "Who has the time or the energy? Someday when I'm sitting on the porch in my rocking chair I'll recount the whole thing, but right now I'm too busy living it."

Living it, yes. But understanding it? I don't think so. If she ever does write on the porch in her rocking chair the account will be something entirely different. It will be a memoir, not a journal of self-discovery. But I do understand what she means about finding time. There's never enough time as we run frantically from job, to home, to meeting, to church, to social engagement, to appointment, and back again. But I felt this exercise in spiritual expansion was important enough that gradually I worked out a system. I would arrive at work fifteen minutes to a half hour before everyone else did, lock my office door, and begin the day with a reading, a prayer, and a short meditation. The evenings after everyone was in bed were reserved for journal writing and more in-depth reading.

Over time, I learned that there is power in getting in touch with our own wounds. Bearing written witness to our lives strips away the outer shell of sophistication and introduces us to our real selves. It's a humbling thing to face our own vulnerabilities, but it's wondrous and exciting too because so much courage is required. The irony is that instead of making us weaker and more clinging, holding our hurts and our hearts in the palms of our hands can give us strength.

THE GIFTS OF THE SPIRIT

"In stillness," writes Marsha Sinetar, "we learn to hear that in us which is deep, loving and wholly guileless." As I began to cultivate internal quiet, these words proved to be another glimpse into the process of spiritual maturity. Slowly my focus began to shift away from me and on to others, especially the elderly residents of the nursing home. Though my years in that job were permeated by the most intense and constant pain of my entire adult life, I was actually perceived by those I worked with as being upbeat, happy, and positive. And the amazing thing is I actually *was* happy, upbeat, and positive, because I learned to stop thinking about *my* needs, *my* wants, and *my* problems every minute of the day. It didn't mean that I wasn't also miserable, frustrated, and disenchanted at the same time. It's just that while I was at work I was able to suspend misery and enter completely and wholly into taking care that people were listened to, provided for, and loved.

The Cinderella myth teaches us to be self-absorbed. It emphasizes our needs, wants, dreams, and dissatisfactions to the exclusion of almost everything else. It would seem that by going inward in hopes of self-discovery we would only exacerbate this self-centeredness, but I found the opposite to be true. Because I opened myself wide to spirituality, I became keenly attuned to the tenderness of heart that is the best part of me, but the part I had kept largely hidden. Tucking a ninety-three-year-old woman into bed for a nap, listening to the same stories again and again from a man whose mind is ravaged by senility, providing endless reassurance to a scared old lady who roams the halls in frantic search of a husband she doesn't remember has been dead for twenty years, and propping up the lolling head of a proud, fiercely angry woman crippled and bent inward by multiple sclerosis taught me perspective. It also revealed the depth of my own inner wisdom and resources and helped me begin, finally, to grow up. I did not come to work at the nursing home by accident. It, too, was part of the process of saying goodbye to Cinderella.

As I dealt daily with the heartbreak of aging in an institutional setting, I learned another thing—to give thanks in all things. Before I ventured down the spiritual path in earnest, I thought thanksgiving was a holiday and something you did in response to ideal circumstances or answered prayer. Never had it occurred to me that it's a way of being. But as I gradually made this discovery, I saw that this lesson applied to marriage too. Even in the midst of disenchantment, it's possible to be thankful for the good that exists right now. Even when we feel he's let us down, it's possible to be thankful for a husband who sports a great beard, does the dishes, picks up a child from gymnastics, and doesn't tell us our hair looks terrible when there's no question that it does. Being thankful doesn't mean ignoring real problems; it just means being aware of small graces.

Disenchantment is a *dis*-ease of the spirit. To try relieving it with a new relationship, a trip to fantasy land, or any other physical remedy is an exercise in futility. We have no choice but to go inward. Once there, we won't find protection from pain, security from the threat of responsibility, or a Prince Charming in the sky. What we will find is something much more substantial: a spiritual foundation upon which to build a trust relationship with ourselves and with a God who is faithfully guiding us where we need to go. We need to leave the land of make-believe where every wish would come true so we can enjoy the adult privileges of autonomy, intimacy, and communion with the divine.

CHAPTER FIVE

Choosing Trust, Accepting Risk
Honoring an Imperfect Union

❧

Sometimes the most momentous decisions are made in a single breath.
"Will you marry me?"
"Yes!"
"Will you sponsor a Vietnamese family?"
"Yes!"
"Will you quit your job?"
Finally, "Yes."

In the gloom of a mid-February morning we glided down the long driveway to the nursing home, Eric driving, me holding the carefully worded and typed letter of resignation like a child bringing home a spelling test marked with a stick-on star. To put it away out of sight would have been to diminish it somehow, give it less credence, perhaps even to risk the words spilling off the page and burrowing to the bottom of my purse to live among the loose change, old shopping lists, Kleenex, and lint.

"There's Gloria," Eric said, pointing to the taupe-colored Honda Accord swinging in to its usual slot at the northwest corner of the building. He glanced over at the letter in my hand. "I could just pull up beside her, fold it into a paper airplane, and sail it through the window. What do you think?"

I laughed. "Trust me—I really am going to do it."

He didn't laugh back. "I guess I'll believe it when I see it," he said.

It had been two-and-a-half years since the day I'd made the first trip up this particular driveway, a year and a half since Eric wanted me to turn around and not look back, to share his confidence that we'd be financially secure again, even without a salary I had to sweat blood to earn. Placed end to end, the reasons I hadn't quit my job would have marched like bricks down both sides of the drive and filled up the huge wide space in between: Moira's going to college in a year and half; I just got promoted; I can't leave Antonina (she's ninety-three and fragile as a tiny wren); I have to wait until after the holidays, after the Jeopardy Tournament, after Pioneer Day; Dr. Bob and Gloria believe in me, I can't let them down; you don't understand, ninety-two families are depending on me; I. . . .

But there was really only one reason, one word; and we both knew it. *Trust*. This, like so many things in marriage, was a matter of trust.

Quickly, I disappeared through the double doors of the building before Gloria could get out of the car. I needed a few minutes alone, a space of silence to think about what I was about to do. I wanted to leave, was *ready* to leave, but I was terrified, too. Leaving meant trusting that we would survive financially, that I would be successful as a writer, that

Eric's business would continue to revive—and, most important, that Eric could be counted on to resume the major share of our financial burden, at least for a while.

Could I trust him to do that? Could I trust him to recognize danger if it lurked again and muster the courage to do something about it? Could I let go of control without turning back into Cinderella?

TRUST—A DAILY DECISION

Whether disenchantment occurs because of a gradual erosion of joy or a single incident that sends us reeling from shock and dismay doesn't matter. One legacy inevitably left behind is the need to rebuild trust, the need to reach beyond pain and doubt and paralyzing fear and believe again in a relationship that let us down. Even after my surgery and the miraculous healing of spirit that came with it, I wasn't ready to make such a tremendous decision. Almost a year to the day later, I was finally able to take the risk.

I use the word *risk* because that's what trusting someone else always is. No matter who they are or how much we love them we have to decide again and again to believe the best of them and to accept their imperfections at the same time. I didn't always know that. Because I believed in fairy tales, I thought I needed only to throw myself once and for all into my prince's strong arms and trust that he would never drop me. But in the early days of my disenchantment, something happened to show me otherwise.

One morning I was sitting at my desk talking to a social worker on the phone when I glanced up and saw an elderly couple, Mary and Frank, standing at the front entrance of the nursing home, having what appeared to be an earnest conversation. Pushing open the heavy door Mary gently led her husband out into the sunlight. "Now just around the circle, Frank," she told him firmly. "That's the rule."

Frank, who had suffered a moderate stroke six months earlier, smiled and nodded benignly until she repeated the warning a few seconds later. Then he became annoyed and shooed her away as though she were a pesky fly.

Chuckling to herself at this obviously familiar display of peevishness, Mary turned to go inside, confident that she could trust him to do no more than take a few turns around the circular walkway. But as she made her way down the hall toward their room, Frank made his own way down the drive toward the heavily traveled road. Through the window, I watched his departure for a moment before reluctantly paging a nursing assistant. Almost immediately, four of them bolted out the door and brought him back while he fought feebly for the simple privilege of walking alone and unencumbered down East Washington Street.

By the time he returned, encircled by his covey of rescuers, Mary was back at the front door. "Oh, Frank," she said sadly, patting his arm, "I always thought I could trust you."

Listening from the open door of my office, the light and warmth of the morning had ebbed almost perceptibly. Frank, I knew, hadn't intentionally violated his wife's trust. He'd simply forgotten by the time he'd reached the drive that he wasn't supposed to go down it. Who can blame him for wanting to keep walking, perhaps to head uptown for a cup of coffee and a newspaper at the Gazebo Restaurant? But this incident, I knew, wasn't just about loss of freedom—terrible though that is. It wasn't just about the horrors of senile dementia, either. The issue was trust in marriage and how much it demands of us in a lifetime.

What I didn't know then was why I felt sad, as though I were longing for something intangible and at the same time impossible to attain. On and off, I'd thought about it all day, but it wasn't until evening when I sat in bed writing in my journal and watching Eric sleep that it dawned on me. *There never comes a point in a marriage where the issue of trust is once and for all settled—a sure thing.*

Like it or not, I'd thought, staring through the open mini-blinds at the black night, *marital trust isn't the ultimate single-shot leap from the plane.* We can't stand once, breathless, at the open door, our hearts thudding wildly in our ears, and jump into the limitless universe. To exercise trust, we must perform such feats of aerodynamics incessantly—even in sickness and hard times and old age. Most of the time, if we're lucky, the parachute springs open, but sometimes, even in the best of marriages, it doesn't.

Months had passed since Mary and Frank modeled a lesson I needed to learn. As I sat in my office holding my letter of resignation, I asked myself again: Was I ready to be a responsible partner in my marriage and realize that trust is an ongoing decision? Had I accepted the fact that I was married to a mere mortal who might not even stay in his saddle, much less whisk me away to a castle where every dream would come true? Could I choose to count on our relationship so our intimacy could grow, and yet resist bringing to it impossible expectations?

My answer was yes. So I took this leap of trust,

quitting my job, and we traveled, my husband and I, deeper into the heart of marriage.

UNEXPECTED LESSONS

During my last month of work it was almost as though we were floating in a protective, iridescent bubble—anything seemed possible. But then almost immediately something happened to challenge my renewed trust in Eric and bring all the old fears and vulnerabilities rushing to the surface again.

On the first Monday I was home, I slipped on a magazine on the polished oak floor of our family room and suffered a compound fracture of my left wrist. Two surgeries in a week (both with general anesthesia), two short hospital stays, and two months in a cast to my elbow seriously inhibited my production of freelance writing. What's worse, the portion of the $10,000 bill not covered by insurance badly depleted the nest egg we'd saved for the day when I became, as we'd jokingly called it, "gainfully unemployed."

This time there was no sense of the miraculous, no healing of spirit following either surgery, only pain, worry, and a constant struggle to let go and let Eric take temporary responsibility for everything from paying the bills to cooking dinner. How ironic it seemed that what I had done so effortlessly for two decades should now be the very thing I struggled with the most! From this latest trial, I came to understand clearly that marriage isn't entirely about sharing responsibility. It's also about shifts in balance and the fact that sometimes it's necessary, even after our security's been threatened, to surrender complete control. But as crucial a lesson in trust as that was, it was nothing compared to the powerful lesson I would learn from Eric's example. As I vacillated wildly between calm acceptance and obsessive anxiety, he seemed to grow daily in strength and resilience.

"Everything's going to be fine, hon," he'd say calmly when I'd spin into a nighttime panic. "I know it. Soon you'll be well, and then you'll make up for lost time. There's no question in my mind that you're going to succeed."

"How can you possibly know that?" I'd cry. "*Look at me!*" Unless Moira or Julie was around to curl it, my hair hung in limp, flat clumps around my face, which was so devoid of color I looked like I'd been powdered in flour. Since the heavy plaster cast limited what I could wear, I lived in jeans and one of two oversized sweat shirts. To make matters worse, I'm a two-fingered typist, so I could work on the computer only by propping my left elbow on a pillow at a weird, exhausting, and painful angle while pecking at the keys with my one "good" finger and the eraser of a pencil. It was *not* a charming sight.

But it's precisely *because* I looked anything but charming, hopeful, and potentially successful that Eric's unwavering faith was so significant. Trust in a spouse means believing—even when appearances scream "Give it up already!"—that the person you love has the wherewithal to slay dragons and leap tall buildings in a single bound, if not now, then tomorrow or the day after that or ten years from now. It is awesome, humbling, and frightening to be trusted that much, especially when experience teaches us that we all stumble on takeoff at times and land flat on our face. But without a leap of trust in our partner, I don't think it's possible to recover from disenchantment.

"But being disenchanted doesn't necessarily mean you don't trust your husband!" a friend argued when I shared this insight. "I've been disenchanted for ten years, but I still trust him. He wouldn't be unfaithful to me if Julia Roberts threw herself at his feet."

Maybe. But trust doesn't concern itself only with sexual fidelity. When we become disenchanted, we don't automatically hire a private detective to check up on our spouse's whereabouts. Instead, we begin to doubt his ability to live up to the golden ideal. We look around at a world gone dim and wonder whether this is the person who can help open the window and let the light back in, or whether a future with him can be counted on to be as drab as army fatigues and as flat as stale ginger ale. We no longer trust him to contribute to our happiness, or security, or hope for the future, or whatever else it is we need on a deep emotional level. One woman who experienced disenchantment during the third year of her marriage told me that she never doubted for a moment that her husband could be counted on in a crisis; what she wondered is whether or not he could provide day-to-day support. What saves us from the debilitating cynicism about the future that leads to divorce is the courage to probe deeper than the disappointment, boredom, and pain of disenchantment to find a more elemental trust—the trust that says, in spite of our mutual imperfections, we're stronger together than we are apart. If we can latch on to this, I'm convinced we can make it back from disenchantment.

In their book *Being Intimate* (Metheun, 1986), John and Kris Amodio make the important point that the first crucial step toward building trust is reaching out. We have to be willing to take a deep breath and say, "Okay, I know there's no such thing as a real-life fairy tale, but I believe in you anyway. I trust that no matter what happens, your intent is to wish me well." This doesn't, however, mean trusting blindly. It would be absurd, and more than a little naive, to hand over our trust to someone we know little or nothing about, or someone who time and again has proven in significant ways his unworthiness of such faith. But if deep in our hearts we know we're married to a man who loves us and wants our good, then it's worth taking a risk on trust.

The key word, of course, is *intent*. We all make mistakes in relationships—even the gurus who write the best-sellers telling us how to energize and revitalize our marriages make them—so it's crucial that we clear away the clutter surrounding the inevitable blunders and get straight to the intent. Did Eric intend to hurt me by not keeping a firm enough thumb on the business? No. Would he deliberately set out to do me harm? No. Does it *really* mean he doesn't love me when he falls asleep while I'm talking to him? When he does cause me heartache, is he revealing his diabolical wickedness, or just his tarnished armor? Can I forgive him for being human, as I hope he'll forgive me? Building trust is hard enough when we believe the best of each other; in an atmosphere of perpetual suspicion and contempt, it's impossible.

TRUST IN THE COMFORT ZONE

What exactly is trust, anyway? Is it simply an abiding belief in someone or something? Well, yes—and no. Psychologists tells us that trust is comprised of three vital ingredients: honesty, acceptance, and respect. In order to understand how they work together to provide the "comfort zone" that enables us to be our truest selves in a relationship, it's important to take a look at each component. Perhaps the best way to do that is to think back on the earliest days of our romance with our present partner.

More than likely, that time was characterized by fantastic highs and heartbreaking lows, a strong desire to please, and a visceral fear that we might not be attractive, interesting, or appealing enough to keep this glorious prince enchanted with us forever. Though that period was wondrously exciting, if we're honest, we have to admit that a lot of the thrill came from a sense of continuous discovery (he likes old movies and chicken enchiladas too!) coupled with the uncertainty of not knowing whether there would be a future together.

"I always tend to forget the anxiety part," a friend laughed when I asked her to take a trip down Memory Lane. "I always remember the good stuff, the stuff he forgets to do now, like pulling out my chair in a restaurant or saying 'I love you.' But the misery was the pits! I was always waiting for the axe to fall. If he called and said he needed to see me, my first thought was that he wanted to break up. It was like living on the edge of disaster all the time."

When we're in a long-term relationship with someone who is committed to us and wishes our good (though he may not always be great at showing it), we don't have to worry about honesty and acceptance so intensely. While it's true that we're often called on to remake the decision to continue trusting in the rightness of the relationship and its potential for growth, it's also true that shared history grants us the freedom to give voice to the peaks and valleys of our spirit, *knowing there's a good chance it will be okay*. It's like when I lugged around that cast for two months. I could look like the wrath of God, say I was terrified of the future, and accomplish very little in a day, and it was still all right; I knew that sooner or later we'd get past it. When we're disenchanted, however, we fail to appreciate the significance of the "comfort zone."

When Julie's second son was sixteen and had only a temporary driving permit, she dropped him and his girlfriend off for dinner one evening at a lovely restaurant on the square uptown.

"The park was decorated for Christmas, and as I watched them walk past the gazebo, holding hands in the falling snow, I felt such an ache," she told me the next morning. "I looked at them and wished that Jim and I could be starting fresh like that, walking with our heads so close together, madly in love and full of dreams and promises. The feeling was so intensely wistful, I had to turn away. But when I got home, there was Jim and he said, 'You look exhausted. Let me call for a pizza,' and it was okay again. Weird, isn't it?"

No, not weird—just poignant and true and all too familiar. So often we yearn for the beginning of love, remembering only the sweetness, while forgetting that, even at its most shining moment, it lacked the deep trust born of genuine knowledge of each other, the unspoken acceptance that allows us each to be real. Honesty and acceptance are the best part of married love but, too often, the things most discounted amid the barrenness of disenchantment.

R-E-S-P-E-C-T

Aretha Franklin spelled it out for us back in 1967, and she was right—we do need "a little respect" in our love relationships! Like honesty and acceptance, this third component of trust grows with knowledge. Unfortunately, knowledge can also be the reason why we show our friends and coworkers more consideration than we do our mate. It's as though intimacy confers a license to wound. Even though we may genuinely believe that the man we married is a prince among men, we often neglect to show it in our everyday transactions. While we wouldn't have dreamed of telling a new love interest that his taste in music is the pits, we have no compunctions about wording it just that way when he becomes our husband. This is one irony of intimacy: While honesty and acceptance seem to grow as we gain deeper knowledge of our partner, respect often declines, at least outwardly.

"You're going to wear *that*?" a friend screeched as her husband came downstairs to go out to dinner. She turned to me and rolled her eyes. "We've been married ten years, and I still can't get him to match a shirt and tie. He's hopeless."

Another night, at a summer barbecue, another friend's husband was the life of the party as he entertained guests with a hilarious anecdote about how his wife had hidden, naked, behind the hot water heater because seconds after she'd impulsively tossed the clothes she was wearing into the washing machine, the meter reader from the gas company came down the basement stairs. With the washer and dryer running she hadn't heard his knock. Never mind that my friend's face turned crimson and she practically choked on her hot dog—it made a great story, and her husband squeezed every drop of humor out of it.

These examples may seem insignificant compared to the deepest hurts in marriage, but they send powerful negative messages that intensify the feelings of disenchantment. When I was at my lowest point I was highly critical of Eric. If he cleaned up the dinner dishes, I zeroed in on the fact that he forgot to wipe the counter. If he was a week late getting a haircut, I'd remark that he looked like a bum. Always, I told him he was too cavalier about money, too inept at shopping, and too lackadaisical about getting Caitie to bed on time. Even though I knew he was caring and kind and that there was nothing he wouldn't do for us, you'd never have guessed it by my actions during that period. Treating him disrespectfully fostered both his resentment and my own and drove us deeper into disenchantment.

Showing respect isn't just about not criticizing or embarrassing our partner, however. It's also about not trying to control him and by accepting the fact that we can't possibly know what's good for someone else in all situations. Recently a woman I know made a gigantic leap of faith when her husband decided to withdraw life support from his elderly mother.

"I never could have done it had she been my mother," she said. "My religious convictions wouldn't have let me. Truthfully, I was shocked at first that he would make a decision that didn't support life. But then I realized that I was imposing my beliefs on him, which wasn't fair. It was his grief, his judgment call, and he had to do what he thought was right."

Sometimes respecting someone else's freedom to choose can be scary because they might make a decision that leads them away from us. But trust is never self-serving; it doesn't come with strings attached or hidden agendas. It's both unfair and disrespectful to not share our expectations and then be upset when our partner doesn't meet them. Yet we often do that very thing when we utter the infamous "If you really loved me you'd know!"

In my Cinderella phase I'm afraid that line ranked right up there with "If I have to tell you it doesn't count," especially in the early days of our relationship. The first year we were married I was hurt because Eric didn't plan anything special for Saint Patrick's Day. The fact that he's German-Swiss and didn't know a shillelagh from a baseball bat didn't have anything to do with it—I was convinced he was taking me for granted by ignoring a holiday that in my family outranks Halloween and the Fourth of July. Crazy, yes, but somewhere along the line I'd picked up the idea that any Prince Charming worthy of the title is a mind reader!

A fellow survivor of disenchantment told me, "Respecting Chuck enough to be straightforward about my expectations has improved our relationship a hundred times over."

"I feel like I finally have a fighting chance," her husband added.

In making the decision to resign from the nursing home, I'd already considered the three crucial components of trust—honesty, acceptance, and respect—without actually being aware of the process. Straight up, I'd told Eric that even though I was quitting, I was scared to death he was encouraging me to do something that ten out of ten financial planners would call an exercise in lunacy.

"I'm doing it," I'd told him. "But not without a lot of trepidation, especially since *you* don't seem to have any."

"I think you have more than enough for both of us," he'd laughed.

He was right—I did—and I felt I had to be honest

about it. The way I saw it, giving up a stable, salaried position to chase a crazy dream on the heels of calamity was not only risky, but downright crazy. I'd just decided to accept it, that's all, just as I'd decided to accept the fact that there are no more guarantees of happily ever after in business than there are in love. But I'd also decided that we had one important thing going for us—mutual respect. Even during our darkest days, we'd never lost sight of the fact that we're both survivors. We learned that we had the wherewithal to land on our feet and that neither of us would just give up. But ultimately we had to look beyond "evidence" and appearances and trust in things unseen—in love and dreams and the elemental belief that together we can do anything.

It isn't enough to ask, Do I trust you? Do I trust myself? The $64,000 question is, Do I trust *us*? Trust *always* entails risk; there are no guarantees. But there can be no meaningful intimacy in marriage unless we believe the best of each other while accepting the worst. Will I honor this relationship I've committed myself to?

Until I could choose once again to believe that this union of two imperfect people was the gift that would continue teaching me what I needed to learn on this earth, I couldn't accept its imperfections. I couldn't enjoy it and relax in it. And I couldn't risk exploring and resolving the next layer of potent emotion: my own anger.

CHAPTER SIX

Cycles of Rage
Anger as an Avenue Toward Intimacy

❦

The anger. If anyone had told me it would bloom like an exotic hothouse flower—huge, blowzy, almost embarrassing in intensity—I wouldn't have believed it. And even if I had, I'd have thought that once life was better it would have disappeared, dropping petal by petal until all that was left was a stalk, a brown and withered thing that I could toss like an old bone into the trash. But that wasn't the way it was at all. Sometimes, even now, it still forms new shoots, blooms again, catches me by surprise.

"Look at this room! It looks like a bomb hit it, and none of you even cares!" I snapped just the other evening. Book bags, jackets, boots, and hats barricaded the door leading out to the porch. The glass top of the coffee table was ringed with soft drink cans, and crumbs from corn chips spread like orange dandruff across the Oriental rug. But Moira sat calmly in the rocker by the fire, watching a *Magnum P.I.* rerun, while Eric and Caitie lay sprawled in the middle of the floor playing Life. No one even looked up.

"See! You don't even care! It's not enough that I have a deadline hanging over my head, Christmas is less than a month away, and. . . ."

"Oh, Mom, it's not that bad. You didn't get so crazed about it last night," Moira said.

"We'll pick up when we're done," Eric mumbled.

"Yeah, later," Caitie agreed.

But the blossom was open then, spreading, a growth gone wild. I jerked open the closet and yanked out the vacuum hose. Too bad if the noise drowned out the TV while the attachment sucked up all those little pink and blue Life people who raced around the game board trying to build careers and fat bank accounts. It would serve them right—the plastic people with their poor priorities and the three real ones who sat out there not caring one whit about my feelings. I'd sweep up every speck until nothing was left—nothing!—but order and calm and some sort of control over. . . .

Over what? Over the three people I love most in the world? Over school paraphernalia, Dorito crumbs, and empty cans of Diet Coke? Or over something else? I dropped the vacuum and rested my forehead against the door frame of the closet. It wasn't the mess in the family room that was causing this fury to flower and expand and press against the walls of my ribs until I thought I'd explode. It was the pressure of not having things done for the holidays, and the two checks I was waiting on for magazine articles, and the fact that today they'd buried a little girl in the Catholic cemetery who'd died in her sleep of an aneurism. I didn't know the family, but had stood transfixed at my living room window watching, heartsick for her parents, scared for myself. What if . . . ? Oh, dear God, what if . . . ?

I shoved the vacuum back inside the closet and went out to the family room. "I'm sorry, you guys," I said. "It's not really the mess. It's just—I don't know—a lot of things, I guess."

Later, when we were alone, Eric asked, "It's Christmas, isn't it?" Every year since the embezzlement, I'd been almost hysterical about the holidays, convinced that it was up to me to make everything perfect, as if I could somehow erase the memory of the horrible Christmas that came right after we'd discovered that the store's books had been "doctored." At that point, we were both settling into jobs we loathed and money was so tight that we didn't even buy each other gifts. My days were filled with sights and sounds so startling and terrifying in their newness that every night I relived them endlessly in dreams. In spite of that, we might have felt the spirit of the holiday had Caitie not gotten the flu and had both the furnace and the hot water heater not died in a duplex we own. Christmas Eve night found us eating takeout Chinese food, while Caitie cried in pain and we tried desperately to figure out how best to pay the plumbing and heating contractor an astonishing $2500.

In response to his question, I nodded. "I just want everything to be good. But I get so scared sometimes. The economy's awful, and here I am without a regular paycheck, and I have so much to do I'll never see my way clear. . . ."

He chuckled and shook his head. Ordinarily, if someone laughs when I'm upset—minimizes my feelings, however irrational they may be—I'm ready to spin into a tirade that makes the previous one look like a minor gust. But that laugh held within it such a depth of understanding, such a desire to reassure, that already I could feel myself begin to let go of the fear.

"It's okay," he said. "It really is. Everything will get done, and what doesn't we'll live without. What counts is that we made it. After three hard years, we're both back doing exactly what we want to do, and we survived. Sure, a regular paycheck would be nice, but the cost is too high. I'd rather be right where we are."

"Me too," I said, and I knew it was true. "But it's not just that. It's the funeral too—the little girl. The thought of losing one of our kids. . . ."

"I know," he said. "I know."

And somehow that, too, was enough.

THE GREAT COVER-UP

It took me a long time to understand that when I'm angriest I'm also the most afraid. Why is it that when all we really want is reassurance and understanding, we demand vacuumed rugs, clean coffee tables, and porch doors that can be opened? It makes no sense, and yet we do it again and again in our relationships. It's even worse during periods of disenchantment, because these are the times when our needs are less likely to be met. We may be lonely, scared, sad, guilty, empty, frustrated, or all of those things, and instead of just saying so, we scream about something as ridiculous as coffee cups left languishing on end tables until green fuzz grows in the bottom.

It's not that we can't legitimately be mad about fuzz-laden coffee cups, but too often, the amount of emotion we expend is out of proportion to the issue. That's because it's safer to turn our wrath on things that are manageable rather than on the real issues that frighten, confuse, and sicken us to the soul. Even when we really *are* mad about green fuzz, the fuzz doesn't fuel our fury so much as the feeling of being taken for granted, of not being cared about enough.

Even now, when I should know better, I'm quick to let anger cover up the truth. The only difference is that now I usually catch myself doing it. But during the bad times, the times when I wanted to say, "I'm scared of what's happening to us," I zeroed in on things that didn't matter and allowed my rage to choke any possibility of intimacy. By the time I had harped about the mundane for an hour, Eric would be just as angry as I was.

"You think you're the only one who's exhausted?" he flung back at me once. "I'm working sixty hours a week trying to keep things together, and I don't like it any better than you do!"

Of course that only intensified the fear that lurked behind my anger, so I got angrier still, until finally he retreated in stony silence. If we're ever to break free of the cycle of pain/anger/pain we have to stop and ask ourselves what need isn't being met. Usually it's a need for closeness, reassurance, understanding, shelter from the storms of the outside world. It's a need felt by both marriage partners, a need we can each fulfill for one another.

So why is it so difficult? Why, instead of sabotaging our own fulfillment by provoking a response that's the opposite of the one we want, don't we just interact in a way that would foster intimacy? Oh, if only it were that easy!

Dr. Herbert Freudenberger and Gail North suggest, in their book *Women's Burnout*, that the reason we get caught up in a cycle of rage is because we don't know *how* to get our needs met. When we're frustrated and afraid, we don't know what to do to be close again. As contemporary women we're busy waging an internal conflict between our dependency needs and a desire for independence, a battle that exhausts and confuses us. So we place most of the burden for "fixing" our ills on our spouse who, chances are, doesn't know how to meet our needs any better than we do. When he fails to support us emotionally the way we want to be supported we feel not only betrayed but outraged, because this failure needles our deepest fears of loneliness and abandonment.

Maybe, we begin to think, the marriage is a sham and his silences are proof that we're just going through the motions. Surely if he *really* cared he wouldn't be insensitive, wouldn't criticize, wouldn't forget to say "I love you," wouldn't shut us out. How could the very same man who stood at the altar and promised before God, family, friends, neighbors, and everyone from the office to love and cherish us forever be so indifferent? Having been spoon-fed fairy tales, we fervently believed that once we found our prince all of our pumpkins would turn into gilded carriages and all of our mice into coachmen. Who can blame us now for feeling so betrayed and angry?

"Betrayal," say Freudenberger and North, "is capable of generating the most direct and explosive outpouring of anger."

Although these authors label our feelings of betrayal and anger "burnout," I think we could just as easily substitute the word *disenchantment*. Either way we feel as though we've been abandoned to our own insecurity and fear. Once we're caught up in the cycle, anger becomes an almost automatic way of responding to anything and everything. We're dying inside of loneliness and misery—our very bones ache with it—but we express our pent-up emotion through harping and nagging. Anger is a scary thing, especially when it zeroes in on the truth. It seems less threatening to shout, "I hate the way you stand in front of the open refrigerator for ten minutes every time you want something to eat," than it is to admit, "I hate the way you shut me out. I'm terrified that you don't love me anymore."

A recent episode of the situation comedy "Empty Nest" portrayed this hilariously and effectively when a central character, Carol, was jealous and hurt that her boyfriend had landed an exciting commission to design and sculpt a piece of art, while the same people who'd commissioned it had passed her by to cater an exclusive party. Initially she went to great lengths to assure him that she was thrilled for him and that he mustn't even think about refusing the offer just because she'd been rejected. But once he agreed with her, she turned on him like a rabid dog. Instead of expressing her hurt and disappointment directly, and realizing that it could coexist with genuine feelings of gladness for him, she launched into a full-scale attack on the fact that his feet were propped up on the coffee table and he was getting eraser residue all over the carpet while he sketched for his new project. One reason it was so funny is because it struck a universal chord. But what's not so funny is the fact that it depicted the behavior most of us are guilty of—the behavior that feeds and prolongs disenchantment.

GAMES COUPLES PLAY

Writing in my journal and taking internal reality checks when I felt my emotions intensify helped me figure out why I could get instantly incensed by something as insignificant as crumbs on the carpet. The bottom line was that I was scared to death we'd never be able to bridge the distance between us, that the world would never again look like a safe and joyful place. I held Eric responsible for the mess we'd gotten into, and I didn't know how to deal with something so potentially explosive. So I didn't. Every time the thought surfaced, I jammed it down and turned my ire on more manageable issues.

When our fear of the ramifications of anger is as great as mine was, sometimes we can't bring ourselves to nag, complain, or shout even about trifling matters. Instead, we take out the smoldering resentment in passive-aggressive ways. We "forget" to take his suit to the cleaners; "accidentally" throw away something important; keep him waiting for half an hour while we get ready to go somewhere, even though we had two hours to shower and dress; make a halfhearted attempt to balance the checkbook and then turn the job over to him with the excuse that we "just couldn't figure it out"; become distracted with the kids' school project while he's relating a story about work; give him the "silent treatment" when he says he has plans to go to a football game with friends; or poke fun at a sensitive issue and then act amazed that he can't take a joke. Forgetting, procrastination, excuses, preoccupation, silence, and hurtful humor create just as negatively charged an environment as nagging and complaining do, but we turn to these "solutions" because we don't know what else to do.

What adds to the problem is the fact that modern society encourages women to get their emotional needs met through games and subterfuge.

Early in life we learn that it isn't "nice" to express our anger straightforwardly. Because I was raised in an Irish-Portuguese household where the decibel level sometimes broke the sound barrier, I'm much freer to vent my fury than many of my female friends. Julie remembers how her mother would retreat to her bedroom with a drink whenever she was angry. Grace recalls protracted silences and banging around in the kitchen. Caroline admits that, just like her mother, she has a tendency to show hostility by running up charge card bills; and Suzanne, a social worker who spends her days counseling people in troubled relationships, says she has to check her immediate impulse to whine or act coy.

It's game-playing. We know it, we abhor it, but still we do it, *even though it poisons our relationships!* Maybe that's because the skewed lessons we learned early in life are repeatedly reinforced, both by the Cinderella myth and by what typically happens during the early stages of romantic love. When we're caught up in the first flush of fascination with each other, both men and women tend to cast a kinder eye on such manipulative tactics, viewing them either as a sign of love or as a red flag warning that the shining dream is in danger of being snatched away if we don't acquiesce to our partner's demands. Women who wouldn't dream of crying on the job or using tears to manipulate their friends don't hesitate to turn on "the waterworks" with their partner. Others withhold sex and/or affection, pout, or throw tantrums—and, at least initially, get what they want.

But the "victories" grow more and more hollow the longer the relationship endures. Every time either partner scores a "win" through manipulation, it's like accruing interest on installment debt.

The one who gives in to save the relationship or keep the peace builds resentment, while the "victor" grows angry and frustrated by the effort that must continuously be expended to get what he or she wants. When this wall of resentment gets high enough, disenchantment is as predictable as the changing of the seasons.

"I've found that as the years go by it becomes harder and harder to get my husband's attention," a woman stated at a marriage enrichment workshop I once attended. "He used to be beside himself to make things right when I cried; now he just walks out of the room, leaving me to get over it—instead, I get furious. I feel so *powerless*. . . ."

"I'm totally impervious to tears anymore," her husband said flatly. "I've given in to so many of them it's a wonder I haven't drowned."

As women, we grow equally disenchanted when we're manipulated by men. Every time we cajole, plead, and scurry around doing whatever it takes to keep him from freezing us out or leveling us with sarcasm we add another brick to the wall of our own resentment. It's the same when we stuff our pain or anger and pretend everything's okay when it's very definitely *not*. By denying our true feelings, we deny ourselves and, eventually, pay the price. We not only become angrier and more disenchanted, we also begin to lose respect both for ourselves and our spouse.

THE INEVITABLE EXPLOSION

Even if you, like me, were frequently exposed to women's expressions of anger while growing up, we aren't usually comfortable with our own angry feelings. We may emulate the behavior we saw in our childhood, but deep down we don't think we "ought" to act that way. It's too bitchy, too shrewish, too unseemly somehow—not to mention too scary and threatening. So we rip into the mundane and keep the real issues and feelings hidden for as long as we can. Never mind that we're so miserable we sometimes sink into depression—we're comforted by the fact that at least it's a manageable misery. Who knows what would happen if we scrutinized the relationship too closely? We think it may be better not to find out.

But sooner or later all this pent-up rage has no place to go but *out*. When the inevitable explosion occurs, we often end up making matters worse by flinging accusations so hurtful that their scars can linger for a lifetime. The night I told Eric I blamed him for what had happened to the business began so benignly that I was appalled by the sudden turn of events, even while they were turning. We had gone out for the evening to a play and had had a good time, until he casually mentioned that, in an effort to build up inventory, the store would no longer be making the payments on our car.

"Oh, great!" I snapped, bursting into tears. "Let's just dig my hole a little deeper, why don't we?"

Six months had passed since the embezzlement was discovered, and all that time I'd been outwardly supportive, even though I believed in my bones that if Eric had listened to my warning and taken action the whole thing could have been avoided. But he hadn't. And now he was finally able to quit his sales job and return to the store, while I was stuck at the nursing home with no end in sight. As usually happens when we've swallowed our anger, my initial outburst was sudden and spectacular.

"It's not fair!" I shouted. "It's not *fair*, and it's all your fault! If you'd just run things better and hadn't been so afraid to take charge of the situation years ago, all of this could have been avoided. But oh, no, you...."

Looking back on that night from a vantage point of several years later, I'm not sorry that I finally told the truth. I *am* sorry about the way I did it. Never did I accept any responsibility for my own unhappiness. Instead I dumped the entire burden on him. I think it was okay to say that I found the situation unfair and that I was miserable in my job. It was also okay to express my anger at him for not being strong enough to prevent disaster from raining down on our heads. But to hold him wholly responsible for my discontent and not share the vulnerable feelings behind the wrath was self-defeating, senseless, and even abusive.

That's the problem with blame. It's a one-horse town to get stuck in. As long as we say "You did this to me" or "You always" or "You never" we're unable to penetrate the heart of the issue. The other person immediately goes on the defensive, and the fight whirls out of control. Fighting is about feelings. It's about the pain, fear, loneliness, and sense of betrayal that gnaws at our insides like a rodent, and until we express our own real emotions and say what we *feel*—rather than what we think or what we calculate has the most power to wound or shock—we accomplish nothing more than widening the chasm between us.

HOW ANGER CLEARS THE PATH TOWARD INTIMACY

When we're honest enough to be vulnerable even in anger, we make a strong statement about our commitment to the relationship. Had I been able to admit that I was struggling with the belief that Eric had played a large part in causing our troubles and that I felt scared, guilty, and sad, I'm sure we'd have ended up in a better place that night. Instead, I hurled accusations like brickbats and cast so much blame that we reached a standstill from the start. I'm not saying that the outcome would have been fairy-tale perfect, but I know we'd have both felt less lonely and alienated and the road to recovery would have been less rocky. Admitting that I couldn't shake the conviction that he was at fault and that I was afraid that this feeling would do serious damage to our marriage would have been a powerful way of saying that I didn't *want* serious damage to occur. It would have been a way of saying "I love you," even while expressing honest, potent anger.

At least ten years ago, a woman told me something so astonishing that I never forgot it. We were standing in the hall of a church talking about an upcoming retreat for married couples when she remarked that she would never consider attending because her marriage was so idyllic there was simply nothing that could be learned.

"In twenty-five years, there's never been one cross word between us," she said smugly. "Never one. We've always loved each other too much to argue."

"Wow," I replied. "That's pretty amazing."

"Yes," she agreed. "But that's the way it is. I'm very lucky."

Although I was a card-carrying Cinderella at the time, I didn't for a minute think she was lucky. What I thought was that she was either lying, deluded, or incredibly naive! Though I was a quarter of a century younger than she, I was old enough to calculate the odds of two people living together for all those years without getting angry. It was as likely as locking starving people in a room with a refrigerator for a week and believing they'd never check out the contents!

Why I remember that conversation so clearly I don't know. Perhaps because it was so ludicrous. But maybe because it discounted the importance of something I knew even then was a part of being married: *As long as there's life, there's going to be conflict.* Like it or not, that's the way it is in nature, in novels, and in marriage. Unfortunately, the concept of "happily ever after" doesn't come affixed with an instruction label, saying, "Important! Angry feelings are an inevitable and normal part of married life. Proceed with caution, but do not assume that anger signals the end of love." Perhaps if it did, we'd learn to deal with our feelings as they arise rather than letting them build up until we're walled off from each other by disenchantment.

This is not to say that allowing ourselves to be angry and to express negative feelings gives us the green light to say anything we want in the name of honesty. We must keep in mind the goal of expressing anger. The goal is certainly not to "win," if by winning we mean devastating the other person with our accusations or making him feel so wretched and guilty that he gives up his own needs and wants in self-preservation. It's not even so we'll feel better, although when anger is resolved we usually do feel less burdened and more hopeful. *The goal is simply to be close again.* The reason we need to express our anger is that it clears a path through the rubbish of pain and misunderstanding so we have room to grow, change, and be intimate.

This sounds so easy, but for most of us it's tremendously difficult because this goal is the opposite of what we've been taught that anger is all about. Most of us have learned that anger is about causing pain, reaping revenge, asserting control, and getting our own way. It takes a long time to incorporate the concept of anger as an avenue toward intimacy. But keeping the goal of anger in mind accomplishes two important things: It encourages us to look behind the anger to our deeper feelings; and it prevents us from launching hurtful, self-defeating accusations that can never be taken back.

Part of the process of dealing with anger straightforwardly is learning to accept the angry feelings that are directed at *us*. Once, not long after I admitted my feelings about the embezzlement, I accused Eric of never sharing his feelings with me. After listening to a torrent of complaints for a few minutes, he leveled a steely gaze in my direction and said evenly, "You don't really want to know what I feel."

"What do you mean, I don't want to know? Of course I want to know! *You* just refuse to tell me."

"Oh, yeah? Well, the way I see it, you hear only what you want to hear. As soon as I say something you don't like, you go into a tizzy. It's easier not to tell you anything."

Ouch! We all claim to want honesty in our relationships, but in order to get it, we have to be ready to hear things we'd rather not, including our partner's anger at us. If we "go into a tizzy"—as my husband rightly claimed I have a tendency to do—we're saying that we need protection from the truth. It's hard to fight fair with somebody who isn't our emotional equal and has to be handled like spun glass.

As hard as it is to learn to use anger well, when

we do, the rewards are sweet. Once Eric and I were arguing about yet another business trip he planned to take. Ever since the embezzlement he'd been traveling extensively to retail shows all over the country in an effort to boost sales. Though he'd been successful, he'd been gone most of the summer. Since May, he'd missed the open house at Caitie's school, Moira's concert, Memorial Day, our anniversary, the Fourth of July, and countless social engagements. Already I knew I'd be facing Labor Day, Band Camp, and the first day of school by myself.

"I can't take this!" I stormed when I heard that he'd be gone an additional fourteen days in a row. "Last week I had an emergency admission at ten o'clock at night and had to take Caitie there with me because I didn't have anybody to watch her. Do you know what that's like?"

"Do *you* know what it's like to live out of a truck?" he retorted.

"I'm sure it's not great. I never said it was. All I'm saying is, this is no way to conduct a life."

He slumped down in a chair at the kitchen table and was silent.

"Well, *is* it?" I demanded.

"Of course it isn't. But we do what we have to do." The words were cold, estranging, like a door that's been slammed and dead-bolted. I felt more hopeless than ever.

"I think I am doing what needs to be done and doing a pretty good job of it too!" I said. "But I'm so tired all the time. I feel like I'm all used up. It scares me to think this is what it's always going to be like." My voice cracked, and I willed myself not to cry.

He looked up at me then, and when he spoke his voice was warmer. "I know. I feel tired too, and a lot of the time when I'm alone in some strange place I wonder if it's all worth it. But we've made enormous progress, and they said it couldn't be done — remember?"

At that I managed a shaky smile. "I just miss you when you're gone," I said quietly, resting my hands on his shoulders.

"I miss you too," he said. "You know that."

The problems didn't miraculously disappear, but suddenly they didn't seem quite as insurmountable, either. Because we'd been able to express the underlying feelings behind our anger, target the one positive aspect of the situation, and express our caring for one another, we felt not only closer, but more willing to look for solutions. It didn't mean that we never fought about the trips again, but I never felt quite so martyred because I knew I wasn't the only one who suffered, and I was learning how to reach across the rage that kept me lonely.

Saint Augustine, who lived in the fourth and fifth centuries, once called anger a weed. Perhaps it is, but it's one that grows in abundance alongside the road leading back from disenchantment. We don't dare ignore it, nor even yank it out and toss it carelessly aside, or else it will propagate a new and hardier species. We have but one choice — to respect the bloom of our anger, learn how to control it, neutralize the acidity of the soil, and use it for medicinal purposes only.

CHAPTER SEVEN

After the Tears
The Grief That Births Compassion

The Balboa Room of the Tucson Holiday Inn was crowded that Friday morning in July. Rows and rows of young people waited to hear what I had to tell them about grieving. Doubt and self-consciousness gripped me as I stood at the podium. What was I doing addressing a convention of Catholic teenagers on a subject I knew nothing about?

I knew about disenchantment, yes; but disenchantment is a far cry from grief. *Isn't it?*

Throughout our ordeal I had never once entertained such a formidable term as grief. To me, it was a word reserved for death and tragedy, a word used only in hushed tones by and about those who had traversed a merciless landscape of pain and tears beyond my comprehension. My friend Kathy had earned the right to use the word when a car traveling down the road in front of her house struck and killed her only son as he rode out of the driveway on his bike.

Compared to her "dark night of the soul," it seemed almost sacrilegious to be standing here talking about anguish. But just as I had been led to apply for the job at the nursing home, I had also been led to accept this invitation. And now it was time to open my heart and let spill from the lessons of loss. I took a deep breath and told this story:

> There once was a village that was attacked and captured by a band of fierce and mighty warriors. The king of the victorious army met with all the village elders and warned them that, unless they appeared at sunrise the next morning with something that would make him happy when he was sad and sad when he was happy, the entire populace would be executed. Immediately, the elders gathered together all the wisest men and women and kept them up all night around a roaring bonfire contemplating this curious conundrum. Finally, daybreak arrived, and the king swaggered into the village, confident that no one would be able to solve the puzzle.
>
> "Well," he demanded. "What do you have for me?"
>
> One of the wise women reached into her bag and brought out a gold ring, which she handed to him.
>
> "A ring!" he scoffed. "What do I want with a ring? I have no use for any more gold. I am a king. I am rich enough already."
>
> "Read the inscription," she replied calmly.
>
> The king held the ring up to the morning light, and a ray of sun glinted off these words: THIS TOO SHALL PASS.

In the two-and-a-half years since the embezzlement my sadness and worry had also passed. Even my friend Kathy had been able to write a book offering promise and hope to other grieving parents. So when I told these kids that God does not leave us to languish in the darkness, I knew I was speaking the truth. Whatever wounded us will more than likely leave its indelible mark on our souls, but somehow, if we learn the lessons of grief, we will laugh and believe and give thanks again. As I continued to talk to the kids, I realized I understood my subject better than I'd thought. Disenchantment had indeed caused me profound grief. It involved the death of a dream—albeit a gossamer dream with no more substance than cotton candy—but a dream that nonetheless promised me abiding fulfillment. To have it snatched away was to be left empty and desolate, to wonder helplessly if the heartache would ever pass.

Sometimes when we talk about the grief of disenchantment we're not taken seriously. Unless the divorce papers are in hand, or the lipstick stains evident on the collar of our husband's shirt, we might be accused of being melodramatic.

"Snap out of it!" well-meaning friends advise. "You think you're the only one who feels that way? That's the way marriage is, so you might as well learn to live with it. Hey, you could have *real* problems. At least your husband comes home every night and isn't abusive. You can't imagine being in my sister's shoes. . . ."

How I wish I had known at the beginning of my journey through disenchantment that if we are hurt, if we feel the sorrow of estrangement and loss, then that sorrow needs no apology or rationalization. Instead, I'd often allowed myself to feel immature and diminished because others could not understand why I had not developed a hard sophistication that either accepts the status quo or begins the search for a new Prince Charming. What I eventually learned is that if our marriage is important to us—and it *should* be important—then to experience the death of its first bloom is to feel the ache of loss.

THE STAGES OF GRIEF

When disenchantment is viewed in the context of grief, all the pain, anger, and feelings of remorse that characterize it begin to make sense. Just as there are distinct stages to be passed through in mourning a death, those same stages apply to other types of grief, including disenchantment. The first stage is shock, when we realize, finally, what it is that's causing our unhappiness. Chances are, we have spent a great deal of time trying to pin the cause of our discontent on everything from career difficulties to our husband's faults, without realizing that our unhappiness stems from the way we've been conditioned to expect marriage to meet our every need.

Once we recognize our disenchantment, we may feel strongly motivated to do something about it. This is the stage at which we read books, make appointments with counselors, initiate discussions with our partner, and talk endlessly to our friends. This occurs because of a driving need to establish order in our lives. Eventually, though, we have to move into the third and most difficult stage where powerful emotions must be faced and worked through. At the most formidable bend in the road, we face our anger and loneliness, confront our fear and, with luck, become willing to move toward forgiveness. What's risky is that we may become bitter and intractable because we find it too difficult to deal with our painful feelings, continue to cast ourselves in the role of victim, or refuse to let go of resentment. But if we accept the inevitable setbacks and keep struggling forward, sooner or later hope will come.

Hope begins in the fourth stage of grief. Usually it springs from external events, such as evidence of renewed trust, the resolution of a long-standing problem, or our partner's willingness at least to try to understand our feelings. But as wonderful as it is to feel that blossom of belief, it's important to remember that the stages of grief are not necessarily consecutive. We usually move back and forth from one to another many times before we reach the final stage, which is acceptance.

Acceptance brings the deepest healing, because it involves the kind of forgiveness that allows us to integrate our painful experience into a meaningful whole. When I was still in my Cinderella mode, I couldn't wait for things to get back to normal so Eric and I could just forget about the nightmare we'd been through and be happy again. By the time I spoke to the group about grief, I had left my job, and Eric and I were beginning a joyful new phase of our lives together. I felt as though I'd emerged from a deep, black hole into a world where people laughed, went on picnics, made lasagna and cheesecake, played driveway tennis, and read books all the way through and knew what they were about. The feeling was miraculous, exciting, wonderful, like being raised from the dead—and I never wanted it to end.

For a while I gave in to the strong temptation to disengage from anything that demanded an emotional price. I didn't want to go back to the nursing home to visit, so I didn't; didn't want to hear about other people's misfortune, so I tried not to; didn't want to do anything more than take care of myself and my immediate little family, so I didn't. It was like a holiday from unhappiness, and I reveled in it. But opening up my wounds for my audience of teens changed all that. I was forced to reacquaint myself with pain and was becoming willing to reach through it to those who might still be on the other side. While there's little doubt that I needed the respite from responsibility that I allowed myself from April to July, the time definitely came to begin giving again. It was time to open my heart and my life in fullness and honesty.

If the experience of grief is to mean anything, then it's critical that we not simply chalk it up as a bad period in life and blithely try to pick up where we left off. If we do, we risk falling into the self-centeredness that lies at the very core of the Cinderella trap. We need to let our grief teach us its unique lessons and carve out new depth and wisdom inside us. The pain of giving up our illusions can introduce us to the privilege of finding peace and joy inside ourselves instead of waiting for it to arrive on a white horse. In order to participate fully in the experience of marriage, we have to bring something to it, and that "something" must be more than physical attractiveness or earning potential, more than good intentions or romantic love—more even than commitment. Grief taught me that marriage requires of us a deep compassion.

THE GIFT OF COMPASSION

Compassion is a gift to the broken, to those who have walked the path of pain and deliverance and, because of it, understand both the flaws and triumphs of love. Compassion gives us eyes to see that for every good in marriage there is a corresponding bad; for every negative, a complementary positive. It enables us to accept that marriage is made up of war and peace, sorrow and joy, estrangement and reconciliation, loss and gain, selfishness and selflessness.

"After you've been through disenchantment and the full cycle of grief, you're different," Julie said recently. "It's like you lose a part of yourself and know you can't regain it, but somehow you're okay anyway. Better, even."

Immediately I thought of a cat we used to have, an enormous black tom named Leo, who bitterly resented the constraints of city living. Every time I would open the door, he'd shoot through it on clawless paws like a plumed dart, eager to do battle with unsuspecting chipmunks. One Saturday morning in the middle of a housecleaning frenzy, I headed toward the garage to deposit some newspapers. Leo was hovering around the door, calculating his odds, so I quickly squeezed through and shut it hard behind me, relieved not to have to jump into the bushes to retrieve him.

"Yeoooooooow!!" The scream was electrifying, unearthly, the quintessential cry of feline distress.

I dropped the newspapers and dashed back inside just in time to see him fly across the kitchen and barrel down the basement steps, howling like a banshee.

Puzzled, I looked down at the floor and saw a trail of blood. Had I caught his leg in the door? Had I scraped him with the storm door? I headed after him, sickened to the soul to think that I had hurt him.

"Mommy!" Caitie called after me. "Mommy, look!"

I turned to see her holding up a fluffy piece of black fur about three inches long. Even before I took it from her, I knew I'd done the unthinkable—I'd cut off the end of Leo's tail!

Cats, we learned, aren't like geckos—their tails don't regrow. But they do mend and grow more fluff and absolve you of the sin of mutilation. After he healed, Leo became his handsome, loving self once again, but somehow he never seemed quite the same to me. There was a sense of lost innocence about him, as well as an amazing display of fortitude and forgiveness.

Trauma, disenchantment, grief—there's no question that they change us forever. But when they cause us to reach deep within our souls to find the treasure of compassion, they become blessings. When I told this to Julie, she nodded in agreement, but also asked a provocative question: "At what point do you stop being compassionate and turn into an enabler?"

For a moment I had no answer. I thought about Eric and me and how compassion had helped me to understand, finally, what the last years must have been like for *him*. Sadly, I can't honestly say that I had enabled him to do much of anything, negative or positive. If anyone had been enabled, I had. For more than two decades, I had been cosseted and protected, enabled to be Cinderella always dancing, dancing, dancing at the ball. But was it really so reprehensible that he should try to give me what I'd thought I wanted? Hadn't he merely done what the Prince Charming myth had taught him good husbands were supposed to do?

"I don't know," I finally answered Julie. "But I think that the knowledge of separateness is inherent in true compassion."

"I think that's true," she replied. "I've learned that when Jim responds to me in ways that seem too needy it's because his wretched childhood is getting in the way. It's something we live with every day of our lives. But I can be compassionate because I've had to deal with my own heartaches. Being compassionate also means that I don't accept responsibility for what only he can come to terms with."

As she does so often, Julie had again clarified my thinking. Compassion for our partner is indeed an empathy with his struggle and foibles, but it derives from the solitary experience of mucking around in our own swamp. No matter how tightly we are joined in marriage, we will always remain separate. Compassion is the shared understanding of this solitary struggle.

A LITTLE LEVITY

Though unquestionably a struggle, I don't think the journey from disenchantment to compassion always has to be heavy, ponderous, and heartrending. I think there's room along the way for a little levity, a healing humor that keeps us humble. Sometimes when we're grieving, we get so caught up in the drama and trauma that we become professional mourners, set apart from the world by virtue of our own sorrow. We forget that our experience isn't that unique.

In *When Bad Things Happen to Good People* (Avon Books, 1981), Rabbi Harold Kushner tells a story about a woman who loses her only son and, overcome with grief, visits a holy man to plead with him to restore her child to life. The holy man listens carefully and compassionately, then tells her she must first bring him a mustard seed from a home that has never known sorrow. Although she visits many houses, the woman can't unearth the needed seed for the simple reason that it's impossible to find a home that hasn't been touched by pain. But she perseveres and ultimately finds something else: the gift of compassion. As she helps the grieving people whose homes she visits, she heals her own grief. What makes this story so insightful isn't just the lesson it teaches about using grief as an instrument for good, but the reminder of how common the experience of grief is. We mustn't take it so seriously, even in the midst of misery or catastrophe, that we forget to weep as much for life's silliness as for its sorrow.

When I first began working at the nursing home I was appalled that my coworkers could laugh at incidents I viewed as unbearably sad. But as time passed and I began to know the residents as people, to love and care for them and to acknowledge my own brokenness, I began to realize that laughter is one of the many faces of compassion, a way of saying, "We're all in this strange, perplexing business of life together!"

A perfect example is an incident starring an elderly lady named Elizabeth whose short-term memory loss was nothing short of astonishing. Notorious for not being able to find her room if she so much as stepped out in the hall and turned sideways, she was nonetheless capable of zeroing in like a homing pigeon on the candy in my office. As many as twenty times a day she'd open my door, shuffle in on enormous pink fuzzy slippers, and say, "Honey, I can't find my room, and I'm a little bit hungry."

"Two-sixteen, Elizabeth," I'd answer with her room number, automatically handing her a blue mint from the jar on my desk and pointing her in the right direction. "Two-sixteen, Elizabeth" became as stock a phrase as "I'll get back to you on that."

One evening when I was working late, I called Eric

to tell him what time to expect me. "I'm almost done," I said. "I would have been home sooner, but. . . ."

Suddenly, shockingly, the door burst open with such force that the doorknob slammed against the brick wall. My framed print of a Victorian house in winter danced dizzily on its nail, and the bowl of sweet annie I kept on the table below it shook as though the tremor had registered a solid five on the Richter scale. Even though a short wall next to the door blocked my view of the intruder(s), my brain instantly clicked into high gear. For two years I'd been listening to nurses and aides whispering about things like this. No doubt about it—I was about to be accosted by *drug thieves*!

Yelping in mortal terror, I flew off my chair and frantically gauged the distance to the bathroom. Did I dare make a dash for it and lock myself in? Surely Eric would call the police and tell them his wife was being held captive in a nursing home by a band of crazed addicts. . . .

Flinging the telephone receiver like a hot poker, I dived for it, banged my knee on the open desk drawer, lost my balance, and wound up sprawled over top of it. Meanwhile, the receiver arced over the top of the desk, hit the metal file cabinet, resonated like a Chinese gong, and landed with a dull thud on the floor.

As I struggled up out of the manila file folders, a familiar squeaky voice asked, "Whatsa matter, honey? I scare you? I'm so sorry, but I can't find my room, and I'm a little bit. . . ."

Before she could say "hungry," or I could get to my feet, from somewhere under the desk a deep male voice roared, "*Two-sixteen, Elizabeth! Two-sixteen!*"

For a second I was as stunned as Elizabeth. But

then I laughed until all I could do was collapse in the chair.

"It wasn't *that* funny!" I heard Eric say from the floor, and I laughed even harder. I laughed until I cried, and it had as much to do with love and compassion as it did with comedy.

By the time this event took place, my Cinderella self had somehow gotten the message that I wasn't the only one who was fractured and bruised by what had happened to us. Eric felt every bit as guilty, worried, and sad as I did, but because he knew how hard my days were, he put aside his own angst and made me laugh. He also knew that I cared very much about Elizabeth and that I knew him well enough to understand that he wasn't minimizing the tragedy of senility.

Laughter helps. It helps a lot. As we work through the dreariness of disenchantment and grief, humor can help heal our hurts and bolster our hope. Every time I think about the night Elizabeth scared me, I marvel at the human spirit and our ability to find humor amid the ashes, to celebrate in the presence of sorrow. In fact, the Elizabeth story has become a stock joke at our house. Whenever one of us can't find something, the other will inevitably say, "Two-sixteen, Elizabeth! Two-sixteen!" This reminds me not only of how dear Elizabeth was, but also of how much compassion can reside in one silly little incident. The reason we keep repeating the punch line isn't because of its humor as much as because it has become an "insider's" joke—something that no one but us would understand. That kind of shared understanding is what intimacy is all about. Sometimes we find it most easily when we're not so intense about the search.

CHAPTER EIGHT

Goodbye, Prince Charming
Reclaiming Hope Through Forgiveness

❧

In the twilight of a January Sunday, we walked up and down the streets of Medina's historic district. It was the dinner hour, and through the mullion windows of what Caitie calls "the antique houses," we could see families gathered around dining room tables. As always, I peeked in as we passed, enchanted by the pastiche of architectural styles—Victorian, Western Reserve, prairie foursquare, and Queen Anne. The new upscale subdivisions with their relentless symmetry, sharp angles, and shine hold no charm for me. So when we walk, Eric and I often find ourselves meandering down streets with names like Friendship and Harmony.

I love the imperfection of old things, the worn and battered places where life and hands have touched, smoothed, and sometimes roughened. I also love the idea of being part of a continuum, of traveling a road that countless others have traveled before me.

Perhaps that's why I came to value the residents at the nursing home so much. I'm sure it's why I came to understand, finally, that love is no more perfect than those old houses with their drafty windows, leaky foundations, and uneven floorboards. But like the old houses, love can endure well and strong and welcoming in spite of its imperfections.

"Oh, look!" I exclaimed, stopping in the middle of the icy sidewalk to admire a small, gray bungalow set close to the street. A big bay window and a narrow porch with a white gingerbread swing gave it the look of a storybook cottage. "I've never noticed this house before, have you?"

"One of these days you're going to get arrested for being a peeping Tom," Eric laughed, pulling me down the darkening street. Almost every time we go for a nighttime walk he says that, and almost every time I'm slightly annoyed that he doesn't share my delight in architectural details and glimpses of stolen domesticity. But on this night I didn't protest as I usually do. Instead I followed his tracks through the hard-packed snow, warmed and gladdened by my expectation of his teasing. An odd thought occurred to me then—*I am content in the commonplace.*

"You know," I said suddenly, "I feel really good."

"I'm glad," he replied. "I do too."

For several weeks I'd been aware of a slight internal shift, a sense of stone moving away from stone to create a space for light. When I said I felt good I wasn't referring to my pleasure in the sight of the first evening stars, or in the luminescence of the snow, or the glow of the houses, or even in the fact that we were holding hands and heading toward home, where a pot of homemade chicken soup simmered on the stove. All of a sudden it seemed crucial that he understand that.

"What I mean is, I feel. . . ." *Joyful, content, peaceful, hopeful.* All of those things, but none of them was quite right.

"Feel what?"

"Forgiving," I said, surprising myself.

Yes, forgiving. That was it exactly. All day the words of an old Shaker hymn had drifted through my head—*'tis a gift to be simple; 'tis a gift to be free.* . . . I'd found myself singing them as I'd toasted bagels for breakfast and thinking of them later at the grocery store while standing idly in the check-out line to buy celery and onions for the soup. *Now, where did that come from?* I'd even asked myself.

The song reminded me of a time almost a year before, when the rector of our Episcopal church had sung it at the nursing home to the most profoundly confused residents, the ones so often forgotten by traveling ministers. When he'd reached the part about turning "to come 'round right," he'd spun slowly in a circle and a hundred-year-old woman who was usually unresponsive had begun to laugh and clap her gnarled hands. As she'd leaned forward in her wheelchair, her face rapt, I'd felt a rush of tears at the surprise, the wonder of such pure, abandoned pleasure. Music, motion, the swirl of gold and white chasuble, an ancient smile—such small joys, such small gifts. *Why*, I'd wondered, *should I think of them today?*

Walking down East Friendship Street with my husband as the moon began to show its shining face, I knew. Forgiveness is also a gift, but more than that, it's surrender from the bondage of disenchantment. Forgiveness allows us to be simple again, to find contentment in the commonplace, to be free of expectation and pain. Finally—finally—I was ready to say goodbye to Prince Charming and welcome my husband into my heart.

LET IT BEGIN WITH ME

Ready is a key word when it comes to forgiveness, because forgiveness is always a decision. As Dr. Paul W. Coleman points out in his insightful book *The Forgiving Marriage* (Contemporary Books, 1989), no matter how badly we've been treated, or even *think* we've been treated, the power to forgive lies not in the person who has hurt us, but in ourselves. No matter what the other person does or doesn't do, we can forgive only when we decide to.

The reason we become disenchanted in the first place is because we feel let down. Too often, we mistakenly think that the magic cure for what ails us is solid evidence that the old husband, who grumbles when it's *our* family coming to dinner but expects veal cordon bleu when it's *his*, has been transformed into a new and improved version. But there's no such thing as a magic cure, just as there's no such thing as a perfect relationship. Even if by some miracle he were to realize his shortcomings and suddenly turn into a prince worthy of a crown, we would still have to forgive in order to put the past to rest. Otherwise we go through life wielding it as a weapon or living in a state of constant watchfulness, certain that he'll disappoint us again.

Our temptation is to zero in on the thousand and one ways our partner has betrayed, disappointed, or misunderstood us without delving into our own role in betraying, disappointing, or misunderstanding him. We focus on the fact that he never spends time with us, refuses to share his feelings, withholds affection, never helps around the house, wants us to be the bad guy when it comes to handling the kids. . . . The list of grievances goes on and on and, in the beginning at least, makes us feel self-righteous and absolved of guilt. When we first realize just how disenchanted we are, there's a strange, perverse power in the knowledge that we can forgive or withhold forgiveness at our own discretion. When we've been betrayed, even in subtle or unintentional ways, it momentarily boosts our lagging self-esteem to think that we can use forgiveness as a weapon to retaliate, control our partner's behavior, and safeguard ourselves from further injury.

What's wrong with this reasoning is that it doesn't take into account what we feel when we carry grudges. It also ignores what Dr. Coleman refers to as the "call deep inside our spirit," the call that is at once both exquisite pain and the urge to let go of that pain — the call to forgive. When we don't let go of long-standing anger and hurt we drag it behind us in everything we do. The flowers lose their bright splendor; our work fails to excite us; our senses are even dulled to the precious and precocious nature of our children. We are so closed off from joy and hope that we live life by halves instead of wrapping our arms around it and embracing everything wondrous it has to offer. Forgiveness is not only a gift we give our partner, *it's also a gift we give ourselves.*

FALSE FORGIVENESS

Sometimes, however, in our need to be rid of the pain and anger of disenchantment, we take on forgiveness prematurely. Though I didn't realize it at the time, my initial outpouring of rage and pain after the embezzlement was an important step in the process of forgiveness, one I couldn't have bypassed. The first step toward true forgiveness is acknowledging exactly what transgressions have been committed and assessing the full extent of the damage. In order to do this, we have to feel the full impact of our emotions. I *needed* to rant and rave, cry and wail about unfairness. Those who move too quickly into forgiveness sometimes do so with the hope that they can avoid the lonely abyss of their own torment. But they succeed only in shoving it down into a dark, dank place where it festers, corroding their spirits.

Others are not so much afraid of pain as they are of loss. According to Dr. Coleman, there are three reasons why we fall prey to false forgiveness: the fear of losing love, the fear of losing self-esteem, and the fear of losing control. When we subscribe to the Cinderella myth we're especially vulnerable to all three of these fears, because the fairy tale imparts such a dangerous moral. From childhood we take away from this seemingly innocuous story the belief that romantic love is the only thing that will save us, and Prince Charming is the only one capable of sweeping us away to a place of security and sunshine. We pick up the powerful notion that only evil stepmothers and ugly stepsisters are allowed to be angry and assertive. And we internalize the message that without a man in our lives we have no value.

When we fear the loss of love, we don't see ourselves as worthy of love; we're afraid that, if we allow our partner to realize the full scope of our feelings, he will abandon us, either literally or emotionally. Even though the relationship is no longer joyful and life-sustaining, we tell ourselves that it's better than no relationship at all. I once had a friend who, for the three years I knew her, seethed with rage because her husband constantly criticized her, ignored her feelings, and treated her as though she were the hired help. Most of the time she kept up the pretense of being happily married, but occasionally the stress would become overwhelming and she'd unexpectedly and, usually dramatically, explode. They'd have a huge fight, often lasting for days, until he'd apologize and resolve to change. For a few days he'd make a halfhearted effort, but inevitably would again begin barking orders and expecting her to anticipate his every whim.

"Why do you keep forgiving him when you know nothing's really changed?" a mutual friend once asked her.

"Because I love him," she replied. "And anyway—who else would ever want me?"

The fear of losing self-esteem is much like the fear of losing love—they both spring out of a sad conviction that we aren't good enough. We fear losing self-esteem because we have so little that we're convinced we have no choice but to cling tenaciously to what we do have. We equate forgiveness with goodness and, consequently, believe that by acting as though we forgive even when we're really angry and hurt, we prove that we're mature, generous, and "above" base and petty emotions, such as anger, neediness, and jealousy.

Likewise, when we fear the loss of control, we operate from a position of low self-esteem. Controlling people are the ones most likely to use forgiveness as a weapon. They may dole it out quickly, but always with the understanding that the one being forgiven should be glad to be dealing with someone so benevolent. Forgiveness becomes one more way of taking charge. Controllers secretly believe that as long as they're in a position of strength, even if that strength has no more substance than tissue paper, no one will discover how vulnerable they really are.

"If he really knew me, he wouldn't like me."

Every time we discuss the current man in her life, a friend of mine repeats this worn-out refrain like a litany. Although he's done many things to disappoint, hurt, and anger her, she always "forgives" him immediately because she fears losing him and being compared to his ex-wife who, at least to hear him tell it, neither understood nor truly cared about him. But underneath her sweet, loving exterior, my friend brandishes control like a silver sword. When she lends him money and uncovers business opportunities for him, he becomes more and more dependent on her. Although her unstinting generosity and quick pardons appear to be rock-solid evidence of her giving nature, they also keep him firmly on the hook—exactly where she wants him.

FORGIVING OURSELVES

True forgiveness has nothing to do with fear and everything to do with love. It's like a plant that offers nutrients to feed and nourish its environment and takes in nutrients to feed and nourish itself. The more we love and forgive ourselves, the more we grow in the ability to love and forgive others; and the more we forgive others, the easier it becomes to forgive ourselves. I didn't understand this when I first realized how angry I was at Eric for not protecting our financial future. I thought my forgiveness was contingent on his "seeing the light" and somehow making everything right again. When that didn't happen, I blamed him for everything from the fear that gnawed at me incessantly to not having time to bake bread anymore.

I wish I could pinpoint the start of forgiveness, isolate the exact moment when I decided that I was responsible for my own happiness, but I cannot. The best I can do is pick out a few road marks along the way. An important one is an incident that happened at the nursing home, a lesson about responsibility unwittingly taught to me by a wise eighty-seven-year-old woman who should be writing a book about marriage herself.

One evening I was working late when I heard a knock on my office door. *Oh, no, please not somebody else who needs something!* I thought. Since lunch I'd dealt with a man grief-stricken by his mother's advancing Alzheimer's, a wife who was terrified that her husband might never come home again, an irate family claiming that someone had stolen their mother's nightgowns, a resident who needed tea and sympathy, and another who was crying uncontrollably but couldn't tell me why because of her aphasia. It was a full half hour before I'd discerned that her roommate had hurt her feelings.

"Come in!" I called, looking up from a stack of paperwork.

The doorknob turned, and Dorothea rolled herself into my office. She had spotted the light under my door on her way back from dinner.

"I knew you were in here! What are you doing here at this hour?" she demanded. "It's after six-thirty. Eileen, you should be home with that nice husband of yours."

"Can't," I said. "Too much to do."

She rolled up to the edge of the desk and shook both her head and her finger at me. "Honey, don't you *ever* say that. No work is that important. You stay here too late every single night. Every time somebody needs something around here they always come to you. But let me tell you something—a good man is hard to find!" She laughed to take the sting out of her words.

"That's what you keep telling me," I said, smiling back. Though she was unquestionably one of my favorite visitors, at that moment I wanted nothing more than for her to go to her room and watch *Wheel of Fortune*. I was exhausted and could already sense that she was leading me somewhere I didn't want to go. I shuffled a few papers to give her the hint, but she ignored it.

"I've said it once and I'll say it again, this lateness every night has got to stop. People around here are just going to have to get it through their heads that you're a married woman. Why do you let them do this?"

Why indeed?

"Do you think anybody's going to remember this when all is said and done? You better believe they won't. Honey, you get only one life, one chance. When it's gone it's gone and you'll wish you could have it back, but you won't be able to. I sit here sometimes and I look at you with a whole future in front of you and I think, you're too nice a girl to lock yourself up in a place like this all day and half the night. I may be an old lady, but let me tell you, if only I could have one more day with my husband, one more, I'd give anything I have left. *Anything*." Her voice cracked and suddenly tears began to well up in her eyes and run down the grooves in her face. She groped in her pocket for a tissue, and I thought of the picture she'd once extracted from that same pocket of the big brown house her husband had built for her—the house they'd been married in, the one she'd lived in until the day she came to the nursing home.

"Oh, Dorothea." I stood up and put my arms around her. "I know," I whispered. "I know." And I did know. I'd give just about anything I had for a day like the ones Eric and I used to have before the world turned upside-down. For a long moment we stood there in the silence of the beige and brown room, our arms around each other, thinking about what we each had lost. And then she left and I turned off the light and sat in the dark and cried until I was too spent to do anything but pack up and go home.

Dorothea was right. Time *was* moving rapidly. I was forty years old, Eric was forty-seven; and I felt as hollowed out and empty as if I'd spent every bit of vitality I'd ever had. A large part of my grief and guilt was tied to the fact that my job consumed so much time. But was anyone really asking me to sacrifice completely my family and my own interests, or was I doing it to myself? As I sat there in the shadows watching the traffic move up and down the rain-slicked street, I came face to face with several terrible truths about myself.

Certainly my work was stressful and demanding, but I'd also unconsciously used it as a way of making myself a martyr to prove just how high a cost had been extracted from me by the embezzlement. I also saw clearly that I was a "pleaser," that I drove myself to do better and better because I felt so inadequate that I needed the constant reinforcement of praise from the administration and families to feel good about myself. I honestly cared deeply about the families and residents I ministered to, but I wasn't nearly so wonderful as everyone seemed to think.

Ah, revelation! Important, necessary, but also potentially dangerous. Sometimes when we realize the full extent of our own shortcomings we become so mired in guilt that we can't climb out. When we feel certain that it's impossible to forgive ourselves we wind up over-zealously attempting to "make up" for our wrongs, punishing ourselves relentlessly, and/or attempting to shift the blame on to someone else. While it's absolutely essential to see our faults clearly and to feel genuine remorse for them, unresolved guilt can become a weapon in itself. It can be a way of focusing so much attention on *our* transgressions, *our* faults, and *our* guilt that our partner's needs and feelings become lost in the drama. People who constantly wail about what unworthy, terrible people they are aren't so much seeking to get past their suffering as they are seeking attention.

I don't want to imply that Dorothea's warning magically set me right any more than any other revelations I had along the way did—I still put in many more late hours after it—but it did open my eyes and my heart to the knowledge of things as they really were. It would have been easy, at that point, to have become so despondent over my mistakes and faults that I became overwhelmed and mired in hopelessness. But just as I was growing in my ability to take off the blinders of romantic fantasy, I was also growing spiritually. I was becoming aware of God's love as I felt his presence and recognized the interconnection of all things. We cannot possibly feel the love of God and deem ourselves unworthy of forgiveness.

The act of forgiving ourselves shows great humility, not only because it requires us to acknowledge the ways in which we have failed to love, but because it insists that we *take action* by putting aside negativity and doing something constructive about our shortcomings. In one of her Southern historical novels, author Eugenia Price repeatedly uses the phrase "an obligation to hope." Though I no longer recall the story line, or even the title of the book that contained it, that phrase has remained in my mind for over a decade. During the year of my disenchantment I had ample cause to be reminded of it often. Forgiveness, I believe, is a powerful way of fulfilling the obligation to hope because forgiveness always brings with it a marvelous sense of awakening or opening up. As we feel its first tentative stirring within us, we begin to believe in the possibility of change and to move toward bringing it about.

But in order to reach the point where it's possible to reclaim hope and effect positive change, we need to focus on our strengths as well as recognizing our shortcomings. By looking at the ways in which both we and our partner individually contribute to the relationship, we give ourselves a compelling reason to continue the process, as well as renewed faith in the future of our marriage. Even when I had not fully resolved the issue of Eric's role in the embezzlement, I began, gradually, to be able to laugh at his jokes again, appreciate his belief in my talent, and be grateful for his steadfastness. I could also allow myself to begin to show evidence of the love I felt but had hidden because of anger and fear.

Choosing to live with joy and optimism doesn't mean trading in the role of Cinderella for the one of Pollyanna, a fictional character who tried to see only the good in all situations. This choice simply means opening our hearts and eyes to the good to help us deal with the bad. Laying down our weapons and opening our hearts is frightening, but it's the crucial step toward solid hope that maybe, just maybe, our relationship is going to be worth celebrating again.

BEGINNING AGAIN

While all of this internal work was going on and I was finally beginning to grasp the idea that I could *choose* to be happy, I also began to be able to talk to Eric about my disenchantment without getting angry and blaming him and also without reeling off into a panic every time I heard something I didn't like. Because I hadn't read much, if anything, about forgiveness at that point, I didn't know that all those long walks and talks around the neighborhood had anything to do with forgiveness. If pressed, I would have said they were the first fumbling efforts toward trying to make sense of what had happened.

Dr. Coleman calls the questioning, listening, groping phase of the forgiveness process "the dialogue of understanding." Whether this phase is short or protracted, difficult or relatively simple, it always has a common purpose: to understand what caused the problem and to devise together a plan of action to keep it from happening again. Dialogue is *not* a mission to find glib excuses to explain away the pain of disenchantment and make it easier to forgive. There are truly no shortcuts in forgiving our partner, just as there aren't any in forgiving ourselves. We have to look at exactly how we've been hurt without minimizing the damage, verbalize our feelings, listen to his feelings, and work together to find a way to begin again.

The first time I used the word *forgiving* with Eric was that night last January as we walked in the snow. I hadn't intended to say it and, in fact, had surprised myself when I did. But we must use the word *forgiving* if we're to complete the journey back from disenchantment. Although it's possible to forgive without saying so, the act of claiming the word becomes a commitment to let go of the past. It isn't enough, however, merely to say "I forgive you." We must also say "I'm sorry." We didn't, after all, become disenchanted alone, nor did we have disenchantment done to us. More than likely, we aren't the only one in the relationship who's been disenchanted either.

As Eric and I turned down our street that Sunday evening, the fragrance of simmering chicken soup wafted out the kitchen vent and reached us on the sidewalk—warm and strong and welcoming. Such a small gift, such a simple one.

"Don't you just love that house?" I asked, pointing to a gray colonial with blue shutters and mullion windows. The dining room light wasn't on, so I peeked into the living room window instead, enchanted by the graceful line of tied-back curtains, the fluid arc of a hoop-backed Windsor chair.

"Shall we find out who lives there?" Eric asked.

"Absolutely," I said. "Whoever they are, they have excellent taste."

Together, we turned up the driveway, laughing as we walked past the picket fence and onto the porch, past the two oak rockers and the red bench made from wood that had been a tree when George Washington was alive. For a second we hesitated, listening to the bells of our laughter pealing in the stillness. Then Eric opened the red door, and I followed him inside. It had been a long, cold walk. It felt good to be home.

CHAPTER NINE

Ah, Romance!
The Bitter and the Sweet

❦

"Come out now," Eric urged. "That can wait. I want you to see what I made."

All evening he'd been puttering in the garage while I prepared snacks for the guests who would be arriving shortly to watch fireworks. Ever since we moved into this thirty-year-old house perched on the far edge of a small lake, we'd engaged in the annual Fourth of July ritual at home.

Shortly before ten o'clock, the residents of Timberlake Estates traditionally gather at the water's edge to sit on blankets or lawn chairs to wait for the fireworks display sponsored by the local Jaycees. The grownups chat about taxes and gardens; the children run through the gathering gloom, waving sparklers like dancing stars.

"Come on. I want you to see. I did it for you." Behind his wire glasses, Eric's eyes were bright, eager as a boy's to show me his creation.

Pachelbel's "Canon in D" poured richly into the night through a speaker he'd positioned in the den window. Curious, I followed the music through the kitchen, into the family room, and out the sliding glass doors to the patio.

"What have you . . . ?" I stopped, mesmerized.

All around the edge of the patio and down both sides of the stone path that winds through our small woodland of maples and ivy, four-foot candles stood aflame in handcrafted wooden holders. I couldn't speak, couldn't react. Dazzled, I simply stood there drinking it in as light and shadow danced to the sweet swell of violins.

"Do you like it?" he whispered, his arm around my waist.

Yes. Oh, *yes!* But I could only look at him with glittering eyes and nod. Our guests arrived then, careening around the side of the house, laughing and calling greetings until they, too, were hushed, halted in their tracks by homemade magic. People crossing from the end of Roshon Drive or cutting over from Strawberry Lane stopped, pointed.

"Look!" they cried as we stood there beneath the sequined sky with our children, friends, and family while the music, candlelight, and skyrockets swirled and splintered around us. Later, after we had blown out the candles and joined the groups clustered at the water's edge, I leaned against Eric, content. *This*, I thought to myself, *is romance*. For the rest of the evening, even though we were surrounded by people, it was as though we were entirely alone, joined invisibly by a gift of love.

So often when I have spoken with women about their disillusionment, they've responded with sadness and wistfulness. A young woman named Anne commented, "I know I need to give up the romantic notions that always seem to leave me disappointed, but it's so hard. Part of me doesn't even want to."

Part of me—a big part—didn't want to give up my romantic notions, either. But, like Anne, I became convinced that if I was ever going to develop a realistic attitude about marriage I had no choice but to get my head out of the clouds and forget about romance. I was wrong. The event I just described took place less than six months ago—here, now, on this side of disenchantment.

The truth is, we *need* romance in our responsible married lives to remind us why we're in this conundrum called marriage in the first place. Romance has the power to whisk us away, if only for a moment, from our worries and to bring us light, joy, and playfulness. It transports us to a secret, private place shared only by two, a place where the angels sing and our spirits soar—if only for a moment. It isn't romance that gets us into trouble; it's our perception of it and the grandiose, impossible expectations we attach to it that cause the problem.

"THAT'S WHAT YOU GET WHEN YOU FALL IN LOVE"

In the '80s, *Psychology Today* magazine conducted a survey about romance, questioning both men and women about its importance in their lives and the extent to which they've been satisfied with its fulfillment. An overwhelming number of respondents, 96 percent, rated romance as important to them, but less than half felt they'd experienced much of it. Why is that? I can't help but wonder if it's because we come to the experience of romantic love dragging all the hopes, fears, and unmet needs of a lifetime in a gunnysack behind us.

Even the language we use to describe romantic love speaks volumes about our core beliefs. We not only actually say that we're looking for Prince Charming or Mr. Right, but we talk about being "crazy in love," "blinded by love," "swept off our feet," "head over heels," "over the moon," and "consumed." In the wake of towering love, seemingly we can do nothing but melt into its embrace and follow blindly wherever it may lead. The Cinderella myth with its strong, all-powerful hero and passive, starry-eyed heroine only serves to foster that idea.

Not long ago, I overheard a salesclerk talking to a customer who was obviously an acquaintance. "Shelley and the baby moved back home last Saturday," she said. "Not that it surprises me. I told her when she married him he was a bum, but you know how that goes. Love is blind."

No, argues Dr. Nathaniel Branden, author of *The Psychology of Romantic Love* (Bantam, 1980), love isn't blind at all. Deep down we know exactly who it is we marry. We simply delude ourselves, either because we aren't aware on a conscious level what our needs are or because we'd rather hide from truths about both ourselves and our partner that we find too painful.

By our unwillingness to take off the rose-colored glasses, however, we succeed only in setting ourselves up for disenchantment. When it inevitably arrives, we feel vindicated placing the blame on the "foolishness" of romantic love. Meanwhile, the same society that sold us the Cinderella myth backs up our new belief. "That's what you get when you fall in love," we're told in both song and well-meaning lectures. Yet when our children disappoint us or we become disenchanted with our careers, very few people tell us that having children or working at a career are the cause of sorrow. I find that strange.

Although some psychologists do discount romantic love as immature, Dr. Branden calls it a "spiritual-emotional-sexual attachment between a man and a woman that reflects a high regard for the value of each other's person." How can we have a high regard for someone's person if we don't see clearly all the good, all the faults, and all the idiosyncrasies that make up that person? And how can we have a high regard for a person who is not our equal?

Before I was married and for most of the time afterward, I saw Eric as the finder of answers, the fixer of broken objects and broken hearts, the weaver of dreams and, as I had engraved on his wedding band, "my refuge, my hope, my love." I didn't see the truth until disenchantment forced me to step outside my storybook role: He can make drastic mistakes the same way I can, and I can be strong and wise and fix things the way he does. Though I would have argued vehemently before the embezzlement that ours was a marriage of equals, I would have been wrong. We had not yet walked through the fire together, had not yet tempered the steel that holds us together in the face of our mutual strengths and imperfections. By the night of the Fourth of July I knew without a doubt who I had married, however, and responded to him with a thrill of joy and a profound sense of peace.

Needless to say, we did not reach this place overnight. Throughout the long months of disenchantment we were mostly strangers to romance. Once during that time I can remember being at the movies and somehow, touched by what we saw on the screen, our hands brushed, then clasped, and we looked at each other. For that brief moment, an electrical current jumped back and forth between us, reminding us of a connection that ran deeper even than our disenchantment. But in a heartbeat it was gone again. And I did nothing to bring it back and neither did he. Perhaps if we had reached out across anger and hurt sooner we'd have gotten through disenchantment easier, faster, but we didn't. In our pain we'd forgotten the healing power of romance.

The myth I subscribed to says that in the natural order the prince is the lover, the princess the beloved. If there are to be romantic moments, then he has to provide them. The problem with this line of thought is that when he doesn't, as so often is the case, we're hurt, confused, angry, certain that love has died and we're being taken for granted—and curiously powerless to do anything about it. Thanks to the compelling influence of the popular media, we cling to the idea that romance has to be a four-star production, rather than something that arises naturally out of the give and take of everyday life. Four-star productions like Eric conducted that magical holiday night are wonderful and we need them, at least once in a while; but more than that, we need everyday garden-variety romance. We need to giggle in the pet food section of the all-night grocery at one o'clock in the morning, go to two movies in one day, and sip a soda through a single straw. We need to give each other these small gifts often.

I think I have always been better at the romantic gesture than Eric is. He does feel things deeply; but for me, as for most women, seeing the romance in the ordinary is almost second nature: a kiss in the kitchen, a single white rose cut from the bush in the back yard, afternoon tea with china cups and lace napkins, a card sent to his office. It took me a long time to realize that romance isn't a chess game where we can't make a move until our partner makes one. And neither is romance a tally sheet: *You surprised me with one sack of licorice and told me you love me six times, and I gave you one back rub and told you I love you seven times; whoops, looks like the ball's in your court.*

I have a male friend who used to feel slighted because his wife "isn't the romantic type." He found himself making all the gestures and becoming hurt when she didn't swoon from the pure wonderment of them. After he realized that he knew when he married her that she was more prosaic than he and it's *okay* for her to be that way, he began to give for the sheer joy it brought him.

"I used to think she didn't care," he said. "She's not the type to buy cards for Sweetest Day or call me at work to say 'I miss you.' I was too blind to see that she shows love in her own way. She'll buy a book I've been wanting to read or handle a problem I'd rather not be bothered with. If I'd been struck with this realization sooner we'd have been spared a lot of grief."

Looking at our mate as he really is, rather than as some fantasy prince, is crucial if we're to avoid a lifetime of disappointment. If I were to wait for Eric to call me "honey" or "darling" in front of other people or for him to make all the arrangements for a romantic night out, I'd be waiting until I was too deaf to hear it and too arthritic to go. It's simply not in his nature. Likewise, if my friend Julie were to expect Jim to create a back-yard spectacle of light and music like the one Eric created for me, she would be waiting an eternity. Jim's mind doesn't work that way. But he does leave love notes for her in the instant coffee jar and never fails to hold her hand at the movies. Part of the secret of recovering from disenchantment is recognizing and being grateful *for what is*.

Yet how easy it is to say that and how difficult to do! Every time we flip on the television we see other women being gifted with diamonds, waltzed under the stars, whisked away on cruises, and caught up in embraces so passionate they melt the knobs right off the Sony. Even now after recovering from disenchantment, I admit that there are still times when I look at Eric and see someone as stodgy, unimaginative, and unromantic as my high school world history teacher. A friend's husband will give her a bouquet of flowers out of the blue, and I'll find myself trying to remember when I last received flowers or even a passionate kiss in the kitchen. Sometimes, if I dwell on it long enough, melancholy turns to anger, and by the time I'm with him again I'm like a faulty wire, sizzling and snapping over everything from his mismatched clothes to the fact that he bought the wrong size can of tomato sauce at the grocery. Yet when I had major surgery, that stodgy, "unromantic" person was the one who lay all night on the floor beside me. Don't caring and steadfastness count for anything? Why do I feel the need to diminish him over trifles? Why can't I remember that simple, unadorned caring is romantic in and of itself, that love doesn't always need wings to fly?

THOSE KILLER COMPARISONS

Author Elizabeth Cody Newenhuyse made a point about comparing marriages that has stuck with me since the day I read it. When we open the door to comparisons, she says, we let someone else into our marriage. Even the Cinderella myth would agree that no one else belongs there. Yet, ironically, it's precisely because we're so hooked on romantic myth that we gladly usher ghosts into our parlors.

I remember a supremely silly fight Eric and I got into one Memorial Day after going to the cemetery to place flowers on his mother's grave. Although this is an important ritual in my Irish-Catholic background and seemed to me heartrendingly romantic at the time, it's so foreign to Eric's family that he couldn't even find the grave site and had no idea which section to look in. When we finally did find the headstone, he plopped the flowers down, read the inscription, and was ready to go. I was furious.

"Isn't this just great?" I cried. "You show about as much caring as nothing. If I die you won't care one bit about me, either. I could be dead fifty years without a flower from you!"

Eric was perplexed, amazed. Why would I even care about something like that? Flowers for dead people who couldn't enjoy them were an expression of love? Incredible. But I was primed by a ritual I'd observed for twenty-odd years and the product of romantic movies where distraught husbands flung themselves on the ground in grief. I was also a hopeless pushover for anything that smacked of sentiment. I even knew all the words to "Tell Laura I Love Her"! And so, I unfairly held Eric to a standard so alien he couldn't possibly meet it.

Romantic ideals are killers. Sometimes marriages go through periods that aren't romantic at all. I don't just mean the "divorce periods," either. I mean the countless times when real life gets in the way and we're too harried, harassed, and exhausted to do anything more than mumble "hello" and "goodbye" as we pass each other at the front door.

Logically we know when we marry that we aren't embarking on a perpetual honeymoon, but it's hard to grasp the idea that the workaday world is a sword with two edges. On the one side, there's comfort and solace in knowing that this person sporting the baggy sweat suit and five-o'clock shadow will be right beside us—as comfortable and familiar as a favorite pillow—through cat hair, dirty dishes, mounting bills, and crabgrass. But on the other, the wretched ordinariness of it all can bring on disenchantment.

"A friend was telling me about how her husband slow-danced with her in the kitchen and I found myself bawling like a baby," confessed Katherine, a dental hygienist in her late thirties. "Over Labor Day weekend an oldies station played what used to be 'our song,' and Greg didn't notice even when I turned it up loud enough to blast him off the couch. He just said, 'Turn that racket down.'" But last winter *I* envied *Katherine* when Greg surprised her with a second honeymoon to Hawaii.

When we feel insecure about ourselves and our marriages we crave the romantic gesture like a drug. Second honeymoons, diamond eternity rings, candlelight dinners, sentimental Valentines—all the tokens of love society tells us we must have in the "perfect" relationship become yardsticks by which we measure the depth of caring. But what society handily forgets to mention is that these things are always an exaggeration and sometimes even a falsehood.

THE GREAT ESCAPE

The grandiose gesture and the passionate declaration are the stuff of which memories are made—no doubt about it. But when they are too facile, the tokens and words of romance can become a form of distancing, a way to avoid the complexity of true intimacy. Lovers who are quick to produce the flowery note or the extravagant night out may not be as concerned with fostering intimacy as they are with avoiding the deepest issues of marriage. My friend Grace illustrated this point when she told me that her former husband always resorted to tokens of romance whenever she tried to confront problems in their relationship.

"He thought you could solve everything in bed," she said frankly. "If that didn't work, he'd try roses or jewelry. My friends thought I was lucky, and for a long time I did, too, but then it reached the point where that kind of romance didn't cut it anymore. It took a counselor to point out that Jack used this approach as an avoidance tactic. He wasn't interested in our relationship growing. He just wanted me to get off his back and knew I could be placated with sentimental gestures."

When we or our partner allow ourselves to become "love junkies," we can be tempted to escape real problems through romantic fantasy. While everyone fantasizes to some degree, it's a dangerous pastime, especially for those in the throes of disenchantment. A few years ago, a women's magazine published the results of a survey about romantic fantasy to which 9,500 women responded, 66 percent of whom were married. While 43 percent of the respondents said they daydreamed about themselves and their husband or significant other in various romantic settings, a remarkable 40 percent admitted they conjured up the same scenarios, only with an idealized "Prince Charming." Forty percent also confessed that they were more likely to fantasize about romance than about fame, career recognition, or a different lifestyle. And 45 percent admitted that they frequently read romance novels.[1]

Publishing data indicates that the romance novel industry is not only alive and well, but flourishing. Some twenty-million readers (mostly married women in their thirties who have some college education) spend over two-hundred-million dollars a year so they can read about love-struck heroines and the men who bedazzle them. Teenage girls quickly read (and sigh) their way through series aimed at the youth market and progress to the adult counterparts, often before graduating from junior high.

Paperback romances don't deserve to take the entire brunt, of course, for furthering myths about romance. Even if they magically disappeared from store shelves, I don't think we'd suddenly begin to appreciate the Lothario sitting across from us at our own breakfast table. But I do think these books and their TV counterparts are our grown-up fairy tales, an element of popular culture that sends us distorted messages about love. We read tales of grand passion and selfless devotion and feel cheated. Everybody else, or so it seems, won the prince who leaves them breathless with delight, while we ended up with the one who throws his dirty socks under the bed and buys us a blender for our birthday. When we don't feel loved and appreciated it's tempting to retreat into romantic fantasy—and modern culture provides us with ample fodder for doing so.

For many women, such fantasizing, whether it be about someone real or imagined, becomes a coping mechanism, a bittersweet dalliance that both enhances and assuages the pain of disenchantment by hinting at the promise of what either could have been or might still be. Surely somewhere, a secret voice whispers, there's someone who could care, someone who's worthy of love and trust, someone with whom all our dreams would come true. But even those women who act out their fantasies often find to their dismay that once passion ebbs, the new prince is no more charming than the last. The coach turns back into a pumpkin, and they're Cinderellas in tatters once again.

A forty-three-year-old wife admitted, "I'm married to a great guy, but we've become so settled, you know? I daydream more than I'd like to admit about an old college boyfriend. I fantasize all these surprise reunions in various settings and how our relationship ignites like tinder and . . . oh, it's embarrassing. It really is. But I'll tell you one thing, when I fantasize, I begin to feel more dissatisfied with life than I already am."

Thirty-six-year-old Beth focuses her fantasies on her boss, a man she feels is equally unhappy in his marriage and who has sent her signals that he could be interested in an intimate relationship. "Of course, I would never have an affair with him," she says quickly. "But I think about it constantly. I look at my husband asleep on the couch by eight o'clock, and I think, *Who needs this?* Fantasy's a dangerous thing, I guess, but how do you stop? My boss treats me so wonderfully, and my husband acts like I'm part of the furniture."

Even if romantic fantasy weren't so seductive in terms of tempting us to act out our daydreams, it would still pose a threat to marriage because it takes the focus off the committed relationship. As I admitted earlier, I found myself slipping into fantasy during the darkest days of my own disenchantment. Looking back, I can see now that it only served to heighten my discontent. I was oblivious to any overtures my husband may have been trying to make. I also believe that had I continued to fantasize, the atmosphere in our home would not have been conducive to romance. When I stopped, confronted the real issues head on, and set about dealing with them, only then was I able to respond to Eric with vulnerability, love, and understanding. My eyes and heart were open to enjoy the romantic moments when they *did* come from my real-life lover.

Romance is not a magic panacea guaranteed to assuage our loneliness, heal our deepest wounds, or protect us from our secret fears. Instead, in the words of Oscar Wilde, romance is "a touch of honey." It's sweetness spread over Eric and me on the Fourth of July like a quilt of many colors. Sometimes I take it out to admire its beauty and experience its warmth before folding it away carefully in my memory.

There will be other magical times for us, and plenty of the mundane. There might even be another "divorce time." But I give thanks that, even after disenchantment, we still hear the angels sing and feel our spirits soar—if only for a moment.

NOTE
1. Elizabeth Cody Newenhuyse, "Why Can't He Be More Like . . ." *Today's Christian Woman* (July/August 1990), page 32.

CHAPTER TEN

Buried Treasure
Uncovering a Lasting Love

Not long ago, Julie and I were sitting on her front porch entertaining ourselves with the singles' ads in the local newspaper.

"Listen to *this* one!" she squealed. "Princess, where are you? Single white male, thirty-something, professional, good-hearted, loves life, seeks single white female to fill glass slipper."

"Let me see." I took the paper and read where she was pointing. "Ohhhhhhh, isn't that. . . ." A word immediately sprang to mind, but I caught myself just in time.

"*Sweet!*" she shouted gleefully. "Admit it—you were going to say 'sweet'!"

There was no use denying it. "I can't believe I'd even *think* something like that!" I groaned. "Here I am writing a book warning women about the dangers of romantic fantasy, and what do I do but fall for it hook, line, and sinker."

She folded the paper and grinned sheepishly. "If it makes you feel any better, I thought it was sort of romantic myself. Face it—we've been thoroughly indoctrinated."

She's right, of course. We can know in our heads, and even in our hearts, that romantic fantasy inevitably leads to disenchantment, but the Cinderella myth still dies a hard death. The thought that I'd weathered a long journey of soul-searching and upheaval only to wind up right back where I'd started struck me as almost unbearable. But if my reaction to the personal ad was any indication, it would certainly seem to be the case. Just mention a glass slipper and—*bingo!*—I was wishing there was a pair of size $6^1/_2$Bs lying around.

Embarrassing and disheartening though it is to admit, there probably will always be a part of me that dreams wistfully of a day when Prince Charming will come charging past my word processor on his white steed and sweep me off to a castle in Camelot. Part of me *likes* the idea of being cosseted and cared for. Part of me *wants* someone to fight for me, defend me, protect me, and spread his cape over the muddy path for me to walk. Yes, of course it's immature. My friend Polly even goes so far as to call it "the attitude that ruins your whole life." But the traitorous "damsel in a tiara" who lives deep in my heart wants it anyway.

So what does that mean? Have all the lessons I've learned been merely theoretical? No, it just means that recognizing the folly of romantic fantasy doesn't banish it forever. Nor does growing wiser guarantee protection from the danger of becoming disenchanted again. Almost everyone I've talked with who has gotten past disenchantment and gone on to build stronger, more realistic relationships admitted that she sometimes still fights the desire to seek out Prince Charming for one last dance. New insights and strong resolve are helpful, but a lifetime of conditioning, coupled with the continuous barrage of popular culture, continues to exert powerful influences.

TRIGGER POINTS

"I've been through two years of counseling," thirty-five-year-old Allison told me, "and I still have a tendency to blame my relationship with my husband for whatever's wrong with me. As soon as something's out of sync in my life I hone right in on the marriage. In a way it's depressing not to have evolved more than that. But as my counselor says, it took longer than two years to get this way, and it's going to take longer than two years to change. I think being aware of my thought processes is the only way to turn my attitude around. You have to head off dangerous thinking at the pass."

It's tempting to feel discouraged at the first sign of "backsliding." Changing how we relate in a marriage is an ongoing process, and everybody who has ever said "I do" is confronted with the challenge. When Julie and I realized that we still instinctively react positively to stereotypical romantic imagery, first I felt despair, then a desire to shrug it off as insignificant. After all, I told myself, that silly personal ad didn't have anything to do with me. And yet the feeling it engendered *did*, and I needed to pay attention to that. If we've successfully made the journey back from disenchantment, we know what triggers discontent and what deepens it, as well as what we need to do to bring our focus back where it belongs: on the relationship we have.

My major pitfall is my desire to have it all, to reach for every good thing life has to offer. When my day is stressful, or just flat, I wrestle with dissatisfaction over where I am at the moment. A piece of music, a movie, a novel—anything that touches my emotions and awakens that sense of longing can bring out my vulnerability if the mood is right. So what am I to do? Not listen to music, go to movies, or read books? No. But I do need to stay aware that these things are my personal disenchantment "trigger points." I also need to remember that stepping out of my glass slippers on to solid—though sometimes rocky—ground has put me more keenly in touch with the emotion of sorrow. As I've let myself mourn my losses, my feelings have come alive, and I have no choice but to experience them.

The other night Eric was sleeping and I was propped up next to him, reading. I happened to glance over at him and noticed he was totally zonked, but was wearing what I always call his "Sister Martha Mary smile." It's a cute, mischievous, devil-may-care grin that I noticed the first night I met him and have always loved. Seeing it so unexpectedly, I smiled to myself and gently touched one corner of his mouth with my fingertip. By his reaction you'd think I had set off a bomb in the bed. He jumped three feet in the air, scrubbed vigorously at his face, and mumbled, "What did ya do that for?" before flopping over on to his side so I couldn't do it again. What had begun as a tender moment ended in a sad, quiet loneliness. It reminded me that life's smallest incidents often probe our deepest hurts. And everybody has those hurts. *Everybody.* Knowing that helps keep me on course.

Throughout the process of researching and writing this book, I have been acutely aware that many wives battle far greater disenchantment issues than I have. I've talked with women who are married to men who criticize and demand, withdraw from family life, refuse to support them emotionally, offer little or no help with housework or child care, take no interest in their successes or goals, are chronically angry, or never, ever notice whether they feel loved and cared for. Some women confront critical difficulties like alcoholism, abuse, and infidelity. My intent is not to equate my situation with any of these unarguably more troublesome challenges, but to point out that disenchantment is so endemic in our society that even relatively content, stable marriages sooner or later experience it, sometimes with devastating results. Every time I read the divorce listings in our local paper I can't help but wonder how many are the result of nothing more heinous than garden-variety disenchantment.

Just this morning I read in Dear Abby's column a letter from an unmarried woman in her twenties who wrote despairingly of how many marriages seem to lose their zest almost as soon as they become legal. "Does no one share life's joys and sorrows with love and respect anymore?" she wondered. Fortunately, as Abby pointed out, there *are* people who have beat the odds; I count myself among them. But I do so with the sobering knowledge that if I hadn't realized what damage the Cinderella myth was doing to my marriage and begun working toward change, I might not have been so fortunate. Left unchecked, disenchantment can lead to divorce, emotional distancing, and the eventual death of a love and companionship that might have lightened our days for the rest of our lives. No one can tell us whether our particular relationship can be saved, but unless we're willing to do the dirty work of sifting through the ashes of storybook romance, we won't know if treasure lies hidden there.

LOVE IN A BROKEN WORLD

When I think about treasure I'm reminded of a story my friend Sharon told me once. When her daughters were three and five years old, their favorite uncle contracted a disease that left him blind. Although learning to maneuver through a world gone suddenly dark was both difficult and frustrating, he found joy in allowing his two little nieces to become his "eyes." Happily tugging on each of his hands, they'd lead him across parking lots, up staircases, and in and out of doorways—all without incident.

One Sunday afternoon the family went to a park to get a head start on summer. Crabapple trees in wondrous bloom blew gently in the breeze, swirling a shower of pink petals to the ground. The girls were high-spirited, giggling and running, pulling their delighted Uncle Ben behind them through the flower-fall.

Then—*crack!* The sound roared out of nowhere and froze the children in their tracks. It wasn't until the oldest began to wail that Sharon realized what had happened. In their excitement, the girls had forgotten that their uncle was twice their height and had inadvertently led him into a low-hanging branch. His forehead slammed against the gnarled bark, raising a bump the size of an egg. Despite Ben's quick forgiveness and good humor, the children were inconsolable.

"We wouldn't hurt you for a zillion dollars!" they cried, clinging to his neck. "We love you!"

To me this vignette is treasure, the whistle in the bottom of the Cracker Jack box, poignantly reminding me that few of us escape hurting and being hurt by the ones we love the most. Sometimes serious violations of trust aren't even deliberate. In our stumbling, bumbling way, we do each other damage without meaning to. That damage may be cumulative, or it may be in one major blow; but if there's one thing we can count on in a long-term relationship, *there will be times when love seems to have failed.*

We grieve those times, regret them, learn from them; but if we are to heal from disenchantment, we also let go of them. Grief, perhaps more than anything else, teaches us that marriage is a serious business that has no room for one-dimensional storybook characters. Yet, paradoxically, grief also teaches us to dig up our sense of humor so that the magnitude of the journey back from disenchantment doesn't blind us to the treasures along the way.

The other evening our daughter Caitlin was in our bedroom, looking through my jewelry box. As I came in, she held out a lavender and white art deco bracelet Eric had given me the week before for Valentine's Day.

"Mommy, did you know there are some pearls missing from around this heart?" she asked, pointing out the defect.

"I know, honey. It's an old bracelet. It was made back in the 1940s. That's fifty years ago."

"Yuck. Why would Daddy buy you an old broken thing like this? I think he should have bought you a new one."

I took the bracelet from her and held it up to the light. It was beautiful, heavy, finely crafted, and as old things always are, full of mystery. I loved it and Eric had known that I would. "I really wanted to find something special for you," he'd told me as I'd opened it.

"Don't you think it's pretty?" I asked her.

"Well, kind of," she replied. "But it isn't perfect, you know."

Perfect—that pesky, familiar word again. I ran my finger over the space where the pearls had been. It was a minor gap, but it had jumped out at me even as I was lifting the bracelet from the box the first time I saw it. What Caitie didn't realize, however, is that there's another, even bigger imperfection. A second heart has no pearls left around it at all. The space where they once were is worn so smooth, burnished so completely to the same hue as the filigree metal surrounding it that only a discerning eye would realize it wasn't meant to be that way. Though I may have a jeweler fill in the small, obvious gap with new seed pearls, I wouldn't dream of repairing the smooth, unadorned heart. It's perfect just the way it is. For me, anyway.

As we struggle to close the book on storybook romance it's important that we redefine what we mean by the word *perfection*. Rather than wasting precious time dreaming of a mythical prince who doesn't exist, we're better off taking a hard look at the husband we chose for ourselves and determining what problems in our relationship we need to repair and which ones we can live with. We may find that when we look with new eyes, the marriage that seemed so flawed has more value than we thought.

A certain amount of disenchantment is inherent in every marriage. And how, really, could it be otherwise? Marriage is the improbable act of two people who are so besotted with one another they can't think straight making a decision to share bed, board, roof, closet space, and the TV remote control for perhaps forty or fifty years. Add to the mix jobs, kids, pets, in-laws, friends, hobbies, bills, illnesses, and a myriad of differences known and previously unknown, and suddenly the relationship takes on a whole new dimension. Instead of a romantic idyll, marriage becomes a stunning leap of faith. We need to expect to feel some serious discontent from time to time. We don't, however, have to accept it as a permanent way of being.

My own progress gives me hope. Even though part of me still yearns at times for happily-ever-after, at my core I know that I really don't want to return to fairy-tale romance. It's kind of like winning the lottery. Like most people, I've daydreamed about what I would do if such a sudden, enormous windfall came my way, but I've never bought a lottery ticket because deep down I really don't want to win. I would rather make my way through my own efforts, even if it means ending up with less glamour. That's exactly the way I feel about my marriage. Being mindful of the peril of storybook thinking is something I may have to work at forever, but by doing so, I bring to my marriage more depth, maturity, and tolerance. I'll gladly sacrifice the fairy-tale trappings for substance and endurance.

Thinking about my bracelet and other imperfections reminds me of an odd fact. Both Amish quilters and Iranian weavers of fine Oriental carpets share the custom of working a deliberate mistake into the intricate design of each quilt or rug they produce. Though separated by thousands of miles, vastly different cultures, languages, and religious traditions, they share this curious custom to remind themselves that only God can achieve true perfection. Rather than detract from the value of their work, however, these mistakes only add to the charm. Buyers gladly pay thousands of dollars apiece for them and consider themselves to have acquired treasure. The sooner we take a lesson both from these humble artisans and from those who appreciate their craft, the sooner we will find treasure in our relationships. We may even find that by redefining our terms, we can live "happily ever after" after all—at least most of the time.

Author

Eileen Silva Kindig is a freelance magazine writer who specializes in writing about relationships. She has published over 300 articles in more than twenty-five publications and currently serves as a regular contributor to *Marriage Partnership* magazine, as well as contributing editor to *Today's Christian Woman*. A frequent speaker at writer's conferences, she also enjoys speaking about women's issues, particularly in the areas of marriage, children, friendship, creativity, and spirituality.

She and her husband, Eric, live with their two daughters, Moira and Caitlin, in Medina, Ohio.